SARTRE

MAURICE CRANSTON

OLIVER AND BOYD

EDINBURGH AND LONDON

OLIVER AND BOYD LTD
Tweeddale Court
Edinburgh 1

39A Welbeck Street
London W. 1

First published 1962
Reprinted 1965

Printed in Great Britain for Oliver and Boyd Ltd
by Robert MacLehose and Co. Ltd, Glasgow

WRITERS AND CRITICS

Chief Editor
A. NORMAN JEFFARES

Advisory Editors
DAVID DAICHES   C. P. SNOW

JEAN-PAUL SARTRE is among the most controversial and important of living writers. He is also uncommonly versatile: a dramatist, novelist, journalist, philosopher, psychologist, and political theorist, his various writings have been much discussed in all parts of the world. Yet no critic in any language has hitherto attempted to appraise Sartre's work as a whole. This brisk and penetrating study by a well-known British author effectively fills that gap.

Mr Cranston argues that it is not only the pressures of the cold war which explain Sartre's withdrawal from fiction-writing and metaphysics to concentrate on political drama and sociology; he maintains that the inner contradictions of the existentialist system itself have driven Sartre to a point where he has been able to avoid a radical revision of his own theories, only by dedicating himself, with ever-increasing industry, to the reformulation of Marxism.

Maurice Cranston is a lecturer in political science at the London School of Economics. He is the author of *Freedom, Human Rights Today,* and a standard biography of *John Locke.* He is a frequent contributor on philosophical and literary subjects to the B.B.C. and the periodical press.

CONTENTS

ACKNOWLEDGMENTS

Thanks are due to M. Jean-Paul Sartre for permission to reproduce all quotations from his works.

Acknowledgments are also due to the following publishers in respect of quotations from the works of Sartre: Librairie Gallimard (*Baudelaire, Critique de la raison dialectique, Huis clos, Les Mouches, La Nausée, Situations I, II,* and *III*); Books for Pleasure (*In the Mesh*); Hamish Hamilton Ltd (*The Age of Reason, Crime Passionnel, Iron in the Soul, Lucifer and the Lord*); Alfred A. Knopf Inc. (*The Age of Reason, The Devil and the Good Lord, Troubled Sleep*); Methuen and Co. Ltd (*Existentialism and Humanism*); Methuen and Co. and Philosophical Library Inc. (*Being and Nothingness, What is Literature?*); Neville Spearman Ltd and New Directions (*Intimacy*); New Directions (*Baudelaire, Nausea*); Rider and Co. and Criterion Books Inc. (*Literary and Philosophical Essays*).

Acknowledgments are also due to the following for permission to quote from the works indicated: Professor A. J. Ayer (article in *Horizon*); Librairie Gallimard (S. de Beauvoir, *La Force de l'âge*); Liberal Arts Press Division, The Bobbs-Merrill Company Inc. (A. Stern, *Sartre: His Philosophy and Psychoanalysis*); *The Observer* (interviews 18 and 25 June 1961); Oxford University Press (M. Warnock, *Ethics since 1900*); Editions du Seuil (F. Jeanson, *Sartre par lui-même*); Professor Paul Tillich (talk in *The Listener*); University of Michigan Press (N. H. Greene, *Jean-Paul Sartre*).

The photograph on the front cover is reproduced by permission of Camera Press, London.

M.C.

ABBREVIATED TITLES
USED IN REFERENCES

SARTRE

All page-references not in brackets are to the original French text; all those in brackets are to the English translations listed here. For details of editions cited, see Bibliography (below, pp. 115–18).

A.R.	=	*L'Age de raison* (*The Age of Reason*, tr. E. Sutton).
C.R.D.	=	*Critique de la raison dialectique.*
D.D.	=	*Le Diable et le bon Dieu* (*Lucifer and the Lord*, tr. K. Black).
E.H.	=	*L'Existentialisme est un humanisme* (*Existentialism and Humanism*, tr. P. Mairet).
E.N.	=	*L'Etre et le néant* (*Being and Nothingness*, tr. H. Barnes).
L.P.E.	=	*Literary and Philosophical Essays* (tr. A. Michelson).
M.A.	=	*La Mort dans l'âme* (*Iron in the Soul*, tr. G. Hopkins).
M.S.	=	*Les Mains sales* (*Crime Passionnel*, tr. K. Black).
N.	=	*La Nausée* (*The Diary of Antoine Roquentin*, tr. Ll. Alexander).
Q.L.	=	*Qu'est-ce que la littérature?* in *Situations II* (*What is Literature?*, tr. B. Frechtman).

OTHERS

Dempsey	=	P. J. R. Dempsey, *The Psychology of Sartre.*
F.A.	=	S. de Beauvoir, *La Force de l'âge.*
S.L.	=	F. Jeanson, *Sartre par lui-même.*
Thody	=	P. Thody, *Jean-Paul Sartre, a Literary and Political Study.*

CHAPTER I

BIOGRAPHICAL INTRODUCTION

Jean-Paul Sartre was born in Paris on 21 June 1905. He has seemed to many readers the least "French" of modern French writers. He is so German, one is tempted to say; and so much the Puritan. It is a fact that he is half Alsatian. His maternal grandfather was Monsieur Schweitzer, author, professor of German, and inventor of the "direct method" of teaching foreign languages (through this connexion Sartre is a cousin of Albert Schweitzer of Lambaréné). It was in his grandfather's house that Sartre grew up, for his father, a marine engineer, died of a fever in Indo-China when Sartre was only two. The professor was a hard-living, high-thinking scholar with the lofty brow and ample beard of the Victorian paterfamilias. In Sartre's early life he was no ordinary father-figure, but the personification of a distant and exalted Authority, almost, one might say, the God-figure. Of having no actual living father Sartre was acutely conscious; he later described himself, the Orphan, as the False-Bastard.

His grandfather was also a Calvinist; hence although Sartre himself was, like his father, nominally a Catholic, we should not be astonished to find in his work an approach to moral problems which is, to say the least, alien to Catholicism. However, when the future philosopher was eleven, his mother married again—once more a marine engineer and a Catholic; and Sartre, a rather sickly boy, who had been cared-for by an affectionate German nurse as well as his doting widowed mother, was then removed to La Rochelle, where his stepfather was in charge of the

docks. Sartre thus acquired an early knowledge of French
provincial life, and evidently an early hatred of it also.
Between the ages of twelve and fourteen he was at the
local *lycée*; then, for one reason or another, he was sent
back to Paris to continue his studies at the Lycée Henri
IV. According to his biographer Marc Beigbeder (who
is not always, alas, entirely reliable), Sartre's family
feared "the dissipated atmosphere of the youth of La
Rochelle";[1] another authority, Dr Peter Dempsey, an
Irish Catholic psychologist, nicely suggests that Sartre's
"preoccupation with the problem of [sexual] inversion
began at La Rochelle."[2]

In 1924 at the age of nineteen Sartre became a student
at the École Normale Supérieure. His papers for the
school-leaving certificate, the *baccalauréat en philosophie*,
had been marked only "fairly good," and when he first
entered for the competitive graduate examination, the
agrégation de philosophie, he was failed; but a year later, in
1929, he emerged at the head of the list. Sartre became a
professeur de lycée, teaching philosophy at provincial
schools, first at Le Havre, another seaport like La
Rochelle, and later at Laon in the North-East. His military service was done as a meteorological clerk with the
army at Tours, his poor eyesight having given him ex-
emption from combatant service.

While still at the university, Sartre formed with a fellow
student, Simone de Beauvoir, a union which, though
carefully distinguished from "bourgeois marriage,"
nevertheless became a settled partnership in life. The
autobiography of Simone de Beauvoir, particularly the
second volume, *La Force de l'âge* (1960), gives a full
account of the author's relationship with Sartre, and is
thus a rich source of biographical material. Destined to
become a novelist, philosopher, and sociologist of the
existentialist school only a little less celebrated than Sartre
himself, Simone de Beauvoir was the carefully brought-
up child of an intensely religious—Catholic—father.

Three years Sartre's junior, and second only to him in the examination for the *agrégation*, she became, like him, a *professeur de lycée*, if perhaps an even more unconventional one, in the years before the War.

Their work kept them apart; while Sartre was teaching in one provincial city, Simone de Beauvoir was teaching in another. Depressed by prolonged separations, they seriously contemplated marriage, but finally decided that as they did not intend to have children there was no justification for compromising with their progressive principles; and they never married. Sartre's anti-bourgeois opinions in his early manhood were moral rather than political; in the election of 1935, when the Popular Front Government was returned, he did not even vote; he was then thirty. He was of the Left, but optimistic enough about the passing of the old order and the coming victory of socialism, to leave day-to-day politics alone. Of those early years, Simone de Beauvoir writes in her memoirs:

> We had confidence in the world and in ourselves. Society, in its present form, we were against: but in that antagonism there was nothing bitter; it entailed rather a robust optimism. Man was to be remade; and that creation was to be in part our work. Public affairs bored us; we counted on events unfolding themselves according to our desires without our having personally to intervene.[3]

Later they came both to adopt a different attitude; to maintain, indeed, that intervention in politics is a writer's paramount duty. But Sartre in his youth was more interested in philosophy. Thanks to his grandfather and his nurse, he knew German well, and he went for a year to study modern German philosophy at the Institut Français in Berlin. It was thus that he came under the influence of Husserl and of Heidegger, whom, however, he never met. Sartre's earliest published works on pure philosophy—*L'Imagination* (1936), the *Esquisse d'une théorie des émotions* (1939), and *L'Imaginaire* (1940)—owe more to Husserl, the phenomenologist, than to Heidegger, the existentialist. But in Sartre's most substantial philosophical work *L'Être et le néant* (1943), though subtitled an *"essai d'ontologie phénoménologique,"* there is more of Heidegger's kind of philosophy; and the book is generally regarded as a treatise, indeed as a classic of existentialism. Sartre himself has always been content to be known as an existentialist.

Being an existentialist, he naturally turned to other forms of writing besides ordinary academic essays. His first choice was fiction. In an essay on *Littérature et métaphysique* Simone de Beauvoir suggests that a philosopher who admits subjectivity and temporality is almost bound to become, however reluctantly, with Plato and Hegel and Kierkegaard, a literary artist. For the existentialist, she adds, fiction has a particular attraction, since "only the novel allows a writer to evoke the original *jaillissement* of existence."[4] So it is not surprising that Sartre should have first made his name as a novelist; though perhaps a little surprising that he should have abandoned novel-writing, as he did, at the age of forty-four.

Sartre began writing stories, it seems, when he was only eight or nine, covering "hundreds of pages of manuscript" to enliven his existence, and so affirming, in the words of his friend and most sympathetic critic Francis Jeanson, "qu'il y a toujours quelque chose à faire."[5] His work did not command immediate acceptance by publishers and editors, but in 1937, when he was thirty-two, Sartre was introduced to the most powerful of French publishers, Gallimard. His first novel was accepted by Gaston Gallimard himself, who also persuaded him to change the title from *Melancholia* to *La Nausée*—a title so apt that it is difficult for the reader to imagine its ever being called anything else. One of Gallimard's editors,

Jean Paulhan took Sartre's short story "Le Mur" for his
own magazine *La Nouvelle Revue Française* and passed on a
second story to another editor. Sartre wrote an account
of his first meeting with Paulhan at his office in a letter to
Simone de Beauvoir:

> Paulhan got up; he gave me a copy of *Mesure* and said
> to me "I'm going to give one of your stories to *Mesure*
> and keep one myself for the *N.R.F.*" I said: "They are
> a bit ... er ... um ... free. I touch on questions that
> are to some extent sexual." He smiled indulgently.
> "*Mesure* is very strict about such things, but in the
> *N.R.F.* we publish everything." Then I told him I had
> two more stories. "Well," he said with an expression of
> pleasure, "give them to me. ..."[6]

Sartre's success thereafter was swift and resounding.
"Le Mur" was the most discussed short story of 1938, and
La Nausée the most celebrated novel. Neither won a prize;
for Sartre was even then, as he has remained, too controversial and disturbing a writer to receive the accolade of
the Establishment; but the reading public responded to
the power and originality of his work. At about the same
time, an appointment to the post of *professeur* of philosophy at the Lycée Pasteur in Neuilly enabled Sartre to
quit the uncongenial provinces and to live henceforth in
Paris. Otherwise the material rewards of success meant
little to him, for he had always been, like his grandfather,
an ascetic. Simone de Beauvoir in her memoirs mentions
an occasion when she noticed Sartre sitting quite happily
in an extremely uncomfortable place near Marseilles;
she protests: "Sartre aimait l'inconfort." Simone de
Beauvoir herself, for that matter, can be considered no
sybarite, judging by the account she gives of her way of
living. She never made a home for Sartre and herself.
Long hours at café tables; bleak hotel bedrooms; holidays spent tramping with packs on their backs: such, she
tells us, was their life together. Travelling during school

holidays before the War—sleeping on decks, in mountain-
huts or the open-air, they saw much of Europe outside
France; not only Spain, Greece, and Italy, but also the
cities of the north, such as London and Amsterdam and
Oxford, in which place Sartre, says his companion, was
"so irritated by the traditionalism and the snobbery of
the English undergraduates that he refused to put a foot
inside any of the colleges."[7]

London, however, pleased him; and in her recollec-
tions of one holiday they spent together there, Simone de
Beauvoir gives an interesting summary of their conversa-
tions:

> Generally Sartre would put forward a "theory," and I
> would criticise it, or give it a different gloss; sometimes
> I rejected it and persuaded him to revise it. . . . But one
> evening, in a little restaurant near Euston Station, we
> quarrelled. . . . Sartre, enamoured, as ever, of a syn-
> thesis, tried to define London as a whole. I considered
> his project inadequate, tendentious, and in truth
> futile: the very idea of such an attempt got on my
> nerves. . . . I maintained that reality goes well beyond
> anything we can say about it; and that we ought to
> confront it in all its ambiguity, in all its opacity, in-
> stead of reducing it to the sort of significance that can
> be expressed in words. Sartre answered that if one
> wished, as we did, to possess reality, it was not enough
> to look at things and be moved by them; we must
> grasp their meaning and fix it in language.
>
> What put a strain on our argument was that in
> twelve days Sartre had not understood London, and
> his summing-up left out a vast number of aspects. To
> that extent I was right to challenge him. I reacted quite
> differently when I read the passages of his manuscript
> where he described Le Havre: there I had the im-
> pression that the truth was being revealed to me.
> However, this difference between us lasted a long

time: I held first to life in its immediate presence, Sartre held first to literature.[8]

The description of Le Havre which Simone de Beauvoir mentions here comes in *La Nausée*, where the town appears under the fictitious name of Bouville. Sartre would probably not have caught its atmosphere so well had he not had prolonged experience of living in such a place. Simone de Beauvoir had the same feeling about her own first novel *L'Invitée*, which tells of two middle-aged intellectuals, lovers, who get disastrously involved with a neurotic girl of nineteen; a grim tale of infidelity and homicide. *L'Invitée* is set in Rouen, and such things, she says, "can only be understood in the context of provincial life; it is necessary to have that heavy, stuffy atmosphere for the least desire, the smallest regret to become an obsession."[9]

Sartre himself, as a provincial schoolmaster, was subject to hallucinations. He believed he was being followed by crayfish. Simone de Beauvoir was much troubled then about his state of mind. She found that his spirits improved on their journeys together, but that his condition grew worse when his thoughts turned to such subjects as the international situation or his relationship with a young White Russian girl named Olga who played a large part in both their lives: one may fancy that Olga inspired both Xavière in *L'Invitée* and Ivich in Sartre's *Les Chemins de la liberté*. Simone de Beauvoir describes how Sartre and she once spent a whole romantic night walking through the paths of Venice; and she adds: "Sartre told me later how throughout that night a crayfish had been following him."[10] In time these distressing symptoms cleared up completely, but the memory of them was evidently with Sartre when he was creating, in *Les Séquestrés d'Altona*, the character of Franz, who imagines himself being judged by a tribunal of crabs.

The war itself was the solution of some of Sartre's

problems. Recalled to his post in the meteorological service, he spent the "phony war" in the Maginot Line, writing. In a letter from the Front to Jean Paulhan, he said:

> My work here consists of launching balloons into the air and following them with binoculars; this is called "taking a meteorological sounding." When I've done this I telephone the wind-direction to the artillery officers, who do with it what they please. The younger school files the information; the old school throws it in the waste-paper basket. Both methods are equally valid, as they never fire. This extremely pacific work (I feel that only the carrier-pigeon-keepers, if the army still has any, can have a more gentle and poetic employment) leaves me many hours of spare time, which I am making use of to finish my novel.[11]

The novel Sartre mentions here is his second, *L'Age de raison*. Too outspoken to be published in Vichy or Occupied France, it did not appear until 1945, by which time the author had greatly extended his reputation with his more enigmatic (less transparently Left-wing) wartime productions, *Les Mouches*, *Huis clos* and *L'Etre et le néant*. During the victorious Nazi advance in the summer of 1940, Sartre was taken prisoner, but was clever enough to persuade the Germans to repatriate him within a year for "health reasons." At a medical examination in the camp, he showed his conspicuous wall eye to the German doctor and claimed that he suffered from "troubles de l'équilibre." He assured Simone de Beauvoir that he was determined to escape if he could not get himself released.

As soon as he returned to Paris, Sartre helped to form a "Resistance" discussion circle among his friends, notably those, such as Merleau-Ponty, Cazin, and Desanti, who shared his interest in phenomenology and Marxism. But Sartre had close friends also in the theatrical world, and while he was seeing his philosophical *chef d'œuvre*, *L'Etre et le néant*, through the press, he was also writing for the stage and giving lectures on classical drama at Charles Dullin's theatre school. Sartre wrote his first play *Les Mouches* for Barrault, but Barrault decided he did not want it; so it went to Dullin, who put it on only as a result of an unexpected intervention. When Dullin said the play would entail excessive production costs, a certain Monsieur Néron, reputedly a millionaire, came forward and offered to finance it liberally. Néron was eventually unmasked as a penniless impostor, but by that time Dullin had gone too far with the preparations and rehearsals to cancel the production.

Some people were (and have since been) puzzled that the Nazi censorship should have allowed *Les Mouches* to be acted in Occupied Paris in the summer of 1943, for there could surely be no failing to discern in the author's invention of a "cult of national guilt" in his imaginary Argos an attack on the official ethos of Vichy France. And indeed, after several performances, the Germans did become alive to this, and the production was suppressed. Yet perhaps one should not be wholly surprised if the German mind was, to begin with, diverted by other aspects of the play, metaphysical rather than political; and for seeing in Sartre, first and foremost, a French exponent of an essentially German school of philosophy. *L'Etre et le néant*, which came out in the same year as *Les Mouches*, was manifestly indebted to Hegel, Husserl, and Heidegger. The Nazis fancied themselves to be admirers of Hegel; they had no quarrel with Husserl; Heidegger they had made Rektor of Freiburg University. Why should they be suspicious of a writer who repudiated French rationalism in favour of German phenomenology and existentialism? As for Sartre's purely literary work, his bitter criticisms of French bourgeois life in *La Nausée* and elsewhere could easily be read as attacks on French life as such, or on the Third Republic—as attacks, in a word, on France.

B

But if Sartre had learned much of his philosophy as a student of the German masters, he was to learn lessons of another kind from the experience of the German conquest. Something of this he expressed in a striking essay written at the time of the Liberation:

> We were never more free than under the Nazi Occupation. We had lost all our rights, beginning with the right to speak. We were insulted daily and had to bear those insults in silence. On one pretext or another—as workers, Jews, political prisoners—Frenchmen were deported. . . . And because of all this we were free: precisely because the Nazi poison was seeping in our thoughts, every true thought was a victory. . . . Every instant we lived to the full the meaning of that banal little phrase "All men are mortal." The choice that each of us made of his life and his being was a genuine choice because it was made in the presence of death; because it could always have been expressed in the form "Rather death than. . . ." Everyone of us who knew the truth about the Resistance asked himself anxiously "If they torture me, shall I be able to keep silent?" Thus the basic question of freedom was set before us; and we were brought to the point of the deepest knowledge a man can have of himself. The secret of a man is not his Oedipus complex or his inferiority complex; it is the limit of his own freedom; his capacity for standing up to torture and death.[12]

The experience of the German Occupation was thus of great significance in the maturing of Sartre's thought; it gave a romantic, heroic elevation to a vision of life which had previously been at best stoical. Several of his friends were arrested, deported or killed in concentration camps. Happily Sartre himself had never to submit to any such ordeal. In fact the success of his published works enabled him to give up teaching in 1944 and devote his time entirely to writing. Much of his writing was done in cafés, notably Le Flore in St-Germains-des-Prés, where the proprietor kept a room upstairs for his literary customers to work in when the café itself was closed. Sartre has always been extremely energetic and hard-working; he was readily capable of sitting up half the night talking, and then writing several thousand words the following day.

Sartre is a short, stocky, pipe-smoking man, badly dressed and distinctly ugly, but extraordinarily impressive and compelling by reason of his tense, muscular, urgent and forceful presence; he is a man who seems to burn with intellectual and moral intensity. He has nothing in common with the popular "existentialist" image created by the young admirers who invaded his old haunts in St-Germains-des-Prés after 1944. The cult of beatnik existentialism is a sociological phenomenon for which Sartre himself must not be held responsible. If he can be blamed for anything, it is for uttering apophthegms which serve no less well as slogans for fools than as keys to his own philosophy: life is meaningless, God is dead, there is no moral law, man is a useless passion, the world is a nauseating viscous mess, the bourgeois are *salauds* (swine, dirty dogs or scum)—a man who talks like this is bound to excite the young, the rebellious and the discontented. In truth, Sartre has no comfort for adolescent nihilists. He is a stern moralist who teaches above all things the need to be responsible and mature. He believes that virtue is possible, but difficult; that the world can be changed for the better, but that change demands a resolute effort.

Sartre is also in some ways unusually formal. From the excerpts of his correspondence with Simone de Beauvoir published in *La Force de l'âge* we learn that these two uncompromising enemies of the bourgeois ethos always address each other, with high bourgeois civility, as "vous."

REFERENCES

1. M. Beigbeder, *L'Homme Sartre*, p. 14.
2. Dempsey, p. 23.
3. *F.A.*, p. 19.
4. Quoted in M. Cranston, "Simone de Beauvoir," in *London Magazine*, (May, 1954), p. 65.
5. *S.L.*, p. 119.
6. *F.A.*, p. 305.
7. *F.A.*, p. 150.
8. *F.A.*, p. 151.
9. *F.A.*, p. 351.
10. *F.A.*, p. 282.
11. *F.A.*, p. 440.
12. *Situations III*, p. 11.

CHAPTER II

LA NAUSÉE

Some critics think that Sartre will be remembered as a dramatist, not as a novelist. It is true that he has forsaken fiction. All his short stories were written before the War, as was his one isolated novel, *La Nausée*. His four-volume novel sequence *Les Chemins de la liberté* was abandoned unfinished in 1949, and he has since written only essays and plays. On the other hand, it is arguable—and it is my own opinion—that most of Sartre's best work is his earliest; and one should certainly not disparage his fiction merely because he has moved into other fields. What is more, in his essays on literary theory, Sartre has written hopefully about the potentialities of the novel form; where he has spoken of the theatre, he has described it as an institution ruined by the exigences of its only public, the bourgeoisie.

Sartre's first novel *La Nausée* remains one of the pinnacles of his achievement. It has certain conspicuous merits of form, shape, economy, and design which are lacking in *Les Chemins de la liberté* and other later works. It is also his most compactly "philosophical" work of fiction; everything in it turns upon, embodies or illustrates his theoretical ideas; it is the *pur sang* of the existentialist novel. The book is cast in the form of the diary of one Antoine Roquentin, who is living in the Norman port of Bouville (Le Havre), working on a biography of an eighteenth-century worthy, the Marquis de Rollebon. Roquentin, we might fancy, is a remarkably free man. He is thirty and has a modest private income; he has no family and no job, none of the so-called "ties."

He has travelled widely; he can do what he wants and live where he chooses. "Free" we may want to call him: but Sartre is out to persuade us that Roquentin is not *really* free. He is *dégagé* or uncommitted; and it is one of Sartre's central beliefs that *dégagement* is only a mockery of freedom, is, in fact, a form of running away from freedom.

Manifestly, Roquentin is not happy. (The original title of the novel was *Melancholia*). He has no friends; nobody writes to him; his only conversation is with the casual acquaintances he makes. He once had a mistress named Anny, and although he dreams vaguely of a reunion with her, she has forsaken him, and is in Paris. In Bouville Roquentin's sex-life is limited to pleasuring, without much enthusiasm, the *patronne* of the café he frequents. His days are passed in a kind of dull depression, with intermittent spasms of nausea, vertigo, acute anxiety, and other forms of nervous tension which, in the Sartrian universe, are not so much symptoms of psychological disorder as intimations of metaphysical reality.

He is a tall man, but not, apparently, handsome. He contemplates his face in a mirror, and confides to his diary: "I can understand nothing of this face. The faces of others have some sense, some direction. Not mine. I cannot even decide whether it is handsome or ugly. I think it is ugly because I have been told so. But it doesn't strike me."[1] Later in the same entry, Roquentin writes: "Perhaps it is impossible to understand one's own face. Or perhaps it is because I am a single man? People who live in society have learned how to see themselves in mirrors as they appear to their friends. I have no friends. Is that why my flesh is so naked?"[2]

The part played by Other People in determining one's nature—and indeed one's very being—is something that is given great importance in Sartre's system. Roquentin's trouble is not "loneliness"; he is alienated from reality itself. Yet his awareness of the external world is extremely acute. He feels it on his nerves; and often it sickens him, brings on what he calls "the Nausea."

It is not that any particular objects sicken him. In fact he confesses that he enjoys touching things which disgust some people: "I very much like picking up chestnuts, old rags, and especially papers . . . with a little encouragement I would carry them to my mouth, the way children do. Anny went into a white rage when I picked up the corners of heavy, sumptuous papers, probably soiled by excrement."[3] He still sometimes wants to pick up pieces of dirty paper, but he discovers that he cannot; increasingly he finds he is no longer able to do what he wants to do; he feels his freedom slipping away from him.

The external world becomes more and more unbearable. He tells himself that objects ought not to *touch* him, yet he *feels* them touching him "as if they were alive," "as if they were living beasts." The sensation of Nausea becomes chronic; Roquentin writes: "it holds me . . . the Nausea is not inside me . . . I am the one who is within *it*." Material objects appear to him as gluey, sticky, visceral. He complains that they are all unnecessary, superfluous, *de trop*; they inconvenience him. He wishes they existed in a more abstract way, less strongly, more drily. People, too, are *de trop*, they are "in the way." The same is true of himself: "And I—soft, weak, obscene, digesting, juggling with dismal thoughts—I, too, was in the way."[4]

Roquentin is now on the point of an important revelation. The word "absurdity" is forming in his mind: but he resists words; what he wants is to get a grip on things. One day he is in a public park, gazing at the black root of a chestnut tree. Its blackness, as he perceives it, is not just a colour, it is also "like a bruise or a secretion, like an oozing—and something else, an odour, for example; it melted into the odour of wet earth, warm, moist wood, into a black odour that spread like varnish over this sensitive wood, in a flavour of chewed, sweet, fibre."[5] As he gazes thus at the root Roquentin feels himself "plunged into a horrible ecstasy"; and it is just then that he understands what the Nausea signifies, and hence what existence is. He does not know how to express this understanding in words, but it strikes him that the crucial point is *contingency*: "I mean that one cannot define existence as necessity. To exist is simply *to be there.*"[6]

Some people may well find themselves wondering here: just what is all this fuss about? After all, Roquentin's dramatic discovery that the world is contingent is one that could have been made by any reader of David Hume in the eighteenth century or after. It amounts to no more than the discovery that the laws of science—or of nature—are not iron laws. The future is not bound to be like the past. In nature we observe regularities; but there is no necessary link between causes and effects. The laws of science are not analytically true, like the laws of mathematics and logic. They are based on statistical uniformities. Because they are contingent, they are sometimes wrong and have to be revised.

In all this, one may feel, there is no cause for excitement even, let alone "horrible ecstasy." But if one feels this, one may not easily understand the predicament of Antoine Roquentin or Sartre's kind of existentialism. Roquentin is a man to whom the questions of metaphysics are questions of life and death. In a universe whose laws are contingent, he has no security He says to himself: "If this is so, my tongue may turn into a centipede." In thinking thus he is plainly giving way to an anxious imagination. Strictly speaking, anything is, in a sense, "possible" in a universe which is not governed by necessary laws; but in a universe which moves in a comprehensibly uniform way, where scientific laws are, if only probable, nevertheless reliable, it is a wildly fantastic—even a pathologically morbid—thought that one's tongue might turn into a centipede.

And yet to raise this objection is perhaps to speak too hastily in the language of common sense, or empiricism, or of the Enlightenment. The language and the spirit of existentialism belong to another, and altogether more emotional order, to Romanticism, and indeed, historically, to religion. The first existentialist, Kierkegaard, was a passionate Christian, and it was the purpose of his existentialism to suggest that the proof of Christian teaching could never be derived from rational arguments about the nature of Creation, but was something directly experienced in the lonely anguish of the sinner separated from God. Even in our own irreligious age there must still be millions for whom the feeling of living in a world without a Heavenly Father would be intolerable. Without God they would dwell in darkness. The condition of Antoine Roquentin is akin to theirs. The thought of living in a universe which is not a rigid and predictable system moving according to inexorable laws is to him a terrifying thought. Sartre is an atheist who understands men's thirst for God, and who teaches them that they must learn to live with their thirst for ever unsatisfied.

In dread Roquentin becomes conscious of the unpredictability of the universe; but in passing from his dread to the cause of it, he learns new truths. If the universe is contingent, it is also free. Because contingency is itself the only absolute, it is "the perfect free gift." "All is free," he tells himself, "this park, this city, and myself." Freedom, therefore, is not something to be found in running away from commitment; it is already there, in the universe, in his own conscious being.

This is another of Sartre's main themes: perhaps his most important. If a man is free, it follows that he is responsible for everything. He is not just a cog in a machine, a creature of circumstance or destiny, a puppet, or a robot. Man is what he makes himself; and for what he makes himself he alone is answerable. Responsibility,

again, is not an easy thing to bear, for it brings with it
that most tormenting of all afflictions, guilt.

Part of Roquentin's trouble is that he deceives himself.
He does not want to feel guilt, and he thinks that in
evading responsibilities—in pursuing his uncommitted
way of life—he can escape uneasiness. But there is no
getting away from one's responsibility; it is part of the
nature of things, a necessary consequence of man's free
being. Self-deception, according to Sartre, is a very
common thing; many people live out their whole lives in
what he calls "mauvaise foi." The history of Roquentin
in *La Nausée* is that of a man passing from self-deception
to at least the beginnings of self-knowledge.

Not, of course, that much can change in the space of
this short narrative; though Sartre is an avowed believer
in what he calls "conversion." To begin with, Roquentin
is content to be a scholar, a biographer, the detached
chronicler of another man's life. In conversation he is
content to be a listener. The excitement life gives him is
vicarious. There is, for example, an incident in a deserted
park, when Roquentin observes an old man in a cloak
approaching a little girl of about ten:

He took two steps forward, his eyes rolling. I thought
he was going to fall. But he kept on smiling sleepily.
I suddenly understood: the cloak! I wanted to stop it.
It would have been enough to cough or open the gate.
But in my turn I was fascinated by the little girl's face.
Her features were drawn with fear and her heart must
have been beating horribly: yet I could also read something powerful and wicked on that rat-like face. It was
not curiosity but rather a sort of assured expectation.
I felt impotent; I was outside, on the edge of the park,
on the edge of their little drama: but they were riveted
to one another by the obscure power of their desires,
they made a pair together. I held my breath, I wanted
to see what expression would come on that elfish face

when the man, behind my back, would spread out the folds of his cloak.[7]

It is only when the little girl turns to run away that Roquentin lets the old man know that he is being watched. There is another incident in the Bouville Public Library. One of Roquentin's acquaintances, the "Self-Taught Man" as he calls him, begins absent-mindedly to fondle a boy scout with whom he is sharing a book; another reader, "The Corsican," notices and, scandalised, creates a scene. In the commotion that ensues Roquentin first seizes "The Corsican," then weakly releases him. Afterwards Roquentin wonders why he let him go. He asks himself: "Have these lazy years in Bouville rotted me?"

He is no more purposeful when he goes to Paris to see his former mistress, Anny, who has invited him to visit her. She tells him that she needs him, but it comes out that all she needs of him is to know that he exists; she does not need to be with him; she is now being kept by another lover, an Egyptian. They talk about their past life together; the tone of their conversation is somewhat quarrelsome. Anny says: "You complain because things don't arrange themselves around you like a bouquet of flowers, without your taking the slightest trouble to do anything. But I have never asked so much; I wanted action." Then she goes on to protest that she has outlived herself. Roquentin wonders what to say to her. Does he know any reasons for living? He has never expected much, so he is not as desperate as she. What does she do with her life? She travels. . . . Roquentin sees the emptiness of it. But he tells himself "I can do nothing for her; she is as solitary as I."

"No reason for living": that is another way of putting Roquentin's problem. The world had given him nothing to live for. He has not even asked for a reason. He had found a sort of escape from the problem in writing his biography of the Marquis de Rollebon. "Rollebon," he confesses, "was my partner; he needed me in order to exist and I needed him so as not to feel my existence. I furnished the raw material, the material I had to resell, which I didn't know what to do with: existence, *my* existence."[8]

At the end of the novel Roquentin has another, and decisive illumination; this is perhaps his moment of conversion. He has a favourite record, the American jazz song *Some of these Days*; and the waitress in the Bouville café puts it on the juke-box for him. As he listens, pictures pass through his mind. He imagines a Jewish musician in a hot apartment in New York finding a reason for living by creating this simple little song. And he asks himself: "If him, why not I?" Why should he, Antoine Roquentin, not *make* a reason for living, *give* a meaning to life by doing something creative? By writing? It would be no use his writing another biography, like the Rollebon book, or a history, either, because all history books are about what has existed, and "one existent can never justify the existence of another existent." The book must be something *created* by him. So Roquentin decides to write a novel:

Naturally, at first it would only be a troublesome, tiring work; it wouldn't stop me from existing or feeling that I exist. But a time would come when the book would be written, when it would be behind me, and I think that a little of its clarity might fall over my own past. Then, perhaps, because of it, I could remember my life without repugnance.[9]

Thus *La Nausée* ends. It is a marvellous book. Although the hero's problems are dramatised, everything is worked out with impeccable logic. Each stage of Roquentin's enlightment follows rationally one from the other. All is beautifully ordered: in this, as in other ways, *La Nausée* is clearly a philosopher's novel. In places it is oddly disturbing, because we are made not only to see, but to sense, what it feels like to be Roquentin going through this crisis of his life. Yet it is nowhere a heavy or oppressive book. Even the claustrophobic atmosphere of Bouville is realised with the lightest of touches. Sartre has to some extent simplified things for himself by telling the whole story from the point of view of a single witness, but that witness is keenly intelligent; and however neurotic, never humourless.

We have seen that Roquentin finds a purpose for his life in art, in writing a novel. The moral of *La Nausée* is that everyone must find his own reason for living; but plainly Sartre himself at this stage of his life was thinking in terms of salvation through art. His attack on the uncommitted life is fully mounted in this novel; but his concept of commitment is not yet given any specific political content. *La Nausée* is an existentialist novel; it is nowhere recognisably the work of a socialist.

REFERENCES

1. *N.*, p. 30 (27).
2. *N.*, p. 32 (29).
3. *N.*, p. 22 (18).
4. *N.*, p. 163 (173).
5. *N.*, p. 166 (176).

6. *Ibid.*
7. *N.*, p. 105 (109).
8. *N.*, p. 127 (133).
9. *N.*, p. 222 (238).

CHAPTER III

CRITICAL THEORIES

In an essay entitled *Que'est-ce que la littérature?* published in 1948, Sartre made the point, already somewhat commonplace, that French writers of his generation, having lived through the experience of the War and the German Occupation, had necessarily to produce a "literature of extreme situations."[1] The age had made everyone "touch his limit." Having said this, Sartre went on to make the more controversial claim that all writers of his generation were "metaphysical writers," whether they liked the name or not. Metaphysics, he said, "is not a sterile discussion about abstract notions . . . it is a living effort to embrace from within the human condition in its totality."[2]

Sartre then named Malraux and St-Exupéry as writers of his own generation, because, although they began publishing at an earlier date, they had the same conception of what literature should be. Malraux had recognised that Europe was already at war in the early nineteen-thirties, and produced a "war literature" while the leaders of the so-called *avant garde* of the time, the surrealists, were still producing a "peace literature." St-Exupéry had adumbrated a "literature of construction" to replace the traditional bourgeois "literature of consumption." These had become the guiding ideas of Sartre's own generation.

It might well be objected that Sartre is claiming to speak for a "generation," when he is entitled only to speak of his own *school* of writers. However, this is what he says:

> . . . we were convinced that no art could really be ours if it did not restore to the event its brutal freshness, its

ambiguity, its unforeseeability; if it did not restore to time its actual course, to the world its rich and threatening opacity, and to man his long patience.

We did not want to delight our public. . . . we wanted to take it by the throat. Let every character be a trap, let the reader be caught in it, and let him be tossed from one consciousness to another as from one absolute and irremediable universe to another similarly absolute; let him be uncertain of the very uncertainty of the heroes, disturbed with their disturbance, flooded with their present, docile beneath the weight of their future; invested with their perceptions and feelings as by high insurmountable cliffs. . . .[3]

This paragraph should perhaps be read in connexion with Sartre's remarks about the German Occupation, which I have already quoted: that it brought one "to the deepest knowledge a man can have of himself . . . his capacity for standing up to torture and death."[4] But it is worth noticing that Sartre's concern with "extreme situations" long preceded the War and the Occupation. In the early nineteen-thirties, when, according to Simone de Beauvoir, politics had little appeal for Sartre or herself, they were both much interested in such violent criminals as the "vampire of Düsseldorf" because they believed that "in order to understand something about mankind, it was necessary to scrutinise extreme cases."[5]

The history of Roquentin in La Nausée is hardly an "extreme case"; there is no "standing up to torture or death" in the book, any more than there is any "tossing" of the reader "from one consciousness to another." Sartre's early short stories, however, are more in line with these avowed aims. In Le Mur, a collection published in 1939, one of the stories is about a group of men condemned to death in the Spanish Civil War and being sent out to the firing squad one by one; another is about a

man who dislikes humanity so much that he shoots
people at random in the street; another describes a
woman watching her husband go mad and trying to
enter his world of delusions; a fourth, a remarkable essay
in "existentialist psycho-analysis" is the case-history of a
young Fascist.

It was apropos of these stories that Sartre said to Jean
Paulhan: "Elles ont un peu ... heuh ... heuh ... libres."
And it was of the same collection, in English translation,
that a *Punch* reviewer wrote that "it leaves *Lady Chatterley's
Lover* asleep at the post." This last remark, much quoted
by the English publishers in promoting the sales of the
book, is a singular one. For the English translation of *Le
Mur* has, in fact, been carefully Bowdlerised out of
respect for Anglo-Saxon sensibilities, as are the translations, published by Messrs Hamish Hamilton, of *Les
Chemins de la liberté*.

The most admired short story in Sartre's first collection
is that after which the book is named, "Le Mur." (The
English version has been given the more suggestive title
Intimacy, from one of the less interesting stories, *L'Intimité*.)
"Le Mur" does not touch on "questions en quelque sorte
sexuelles," but it does deal with a man's "capacity for
standing up to torture and death." It concerns the fate of
three Spanish Republicans condemned to death by the
Fascists, and awaiting execution. Two are duly shot after
a tormented night of waiting; the third, Ibbieta, is offered
his life if he will betray the whereabouts of his leader Gris.
Ibbieta is by far the bravest of the three condemned men.
He has passed beyond hope and is fully reconciled to
death, when, as a grim sort of joke against his captors, he
tells them that Gris is hiding in the local cemetery, fully
believing him to be in fact far away. By a coincidence
Gris *is* hiding in the local cemetery. He is captured, and
Ibbieta's life is spared.

Now, although this is the short-story which (with *La
Nausée*) made Sartre's name in France before the War, it

is, in its general outline, the least characteristic of his works. The neat plot with the "ironical twist" at the end belongs to a tradition of fiction which Sartre specifically repudiates. Maupassant might have invented such a plot. It is a technique which is cultivated by what Sartre calls the bourgeois "literature of consumption." What is more, it is logically connected with just that deterministic philosophy to which Sartre is most opposed, namely that of those nineteenth-century pessimists and historicists, who see man as the creature of a merciless fate which deviously outwits and thwarts him whenever he tries to shape his future. The coincidence of Gris being in the local cemetery; the unwished-for reprieve of Ibbieta—such devices are far too typical of the determinist imagination to bear effective witness to a philosophy which vigorously upholds human liberty.

However, there is no denying the compulsive appeal of "Le Mur"; and what chiefly gives the story its magnetism is the naked intense reality of Sartre's account of Ibbieta's feelings in the death cell. The reader is indeed "caught up" and "trapped" in Ibbieta's fear, and Ibbieta's conquest of fear. We are carried to the point where (as Ibbieta recalls):

In the state I was in, if someone had come and told me I could go home quietly, that they would leave me my whole life, it would have left me cold: several hours or several years of waiting is all the same when you have lost the illusion of being eternal. I clung to nothing; in a way I was calm. But it was a horrible calm—because of my body; my body—I saw with its eyes; I heard with its ears, but it was no longer me; it sweated and trembled by itself; and I didn't recognise it any more. I had to touch it and look at it to find out what was happening, as if it were the body of someone else.[6]

Some of the things Ibbieta says here gain their full

c

meaning only in relation to Sartre's whole theory of
being as elaborated in *L'Etre et le néant,* which I shall
presently discuss. Here we may notice how Sartre makes
Ibbieta's loss of "the illusion of being eternal" the origin
of his courage—or stoicism. One is often told how the
expectation of immortality fortifies the Christian soldier
or martyr to face death bravely. In Sartre's eyes, the
doctrine of personal immortality, by taking the sting out
of death, diminishes the heroism of the man who faces it.
The existentialist teaches that death is an end from which
there is no resurrection; it also teaches that in abandon-
ing the sort of *hope* which Christianity breeds, a man may
find in himself the strength to face what is inescapable;
courage, among other things, is found "on the other side
of despair."[7]

Sartre's disagreement with Christian metaphysics is of
considerable importance in view of the fact that existentialism is historically derived from a form of Christianity
and is still allied to Christianity for such theorists as
Jaspers, Marcel and Gilson. Sartre's position in this
matter is nowhere made more clear than in a critique of
the self-consciously Christian novelist Mauriac, which
was originally published in magazine form in February
1939, under the title "M. François Mauriac et la liberté."[8]
This essay, celebrated for its punch—and rudeness—
contains an important statement about the place of
human freedom in the cosmology of the novel. Sartre's
argument is that characters in fiction can only be successful, can only live and be real if they are *free*, if they have
the freedom which human beings in the actual world
have. Otherwise invented characters cannot be interesting or convincing: "If I suspect that the hero's future
actions are determined in advance by heredity, social influence or some other mechanism, my own tide ebbs back
into me; there remains only myself, reading and persisting,
confronted by a static book."[9] Sartre's case against
Mauriac is that Mauriac's notion of predestination leads

him to write novels peopled by puppets. And the doings of puppets, says Sartre, are instrinsically boring.

Sartre provides a close anlysis of one of Mauriac's most famous characters, Thérèse in the novel *La Fin de la nuit*. Sartre asks: is Thérèse free? Manifestly she is not; she is "a witch, a possessed creature." Thus, Sartre continues, this novel is "above all the story of an enslavement." The heroine's "ups and downs affect me little more than those of a cockroach climbing a wall with stupid obstinacy."[10] Mauriac's concept of destiny implies that everything that happens is in principle predictable; whereas, for Sartre, the "real novelist" is stirred by things that are unpredictable; he is "excited by doors because they must be opened; by envelopes because they must be unsealed."[11]

Sartre has another objection to Mauriac. He protests that Mauriac "takes God's standpoint on his characters."[12] And this pretence of an absolute knowledge, says Sartre, involves a twofold error of technique. First, it brings in a purely contemplative narrator, withdrawn from the action which is recorded. Secondly, in Mauriac's case, it has led the author to prefabricate his characters before he sets them down. These characters are, so to speak, *essences*, not *existing beings*. Furthermore, Sartre sees in Mauriac's presumption to the standpoint of God not only an intellectual weakness but a definite moral defect, the "sin of pride." Sartre writes:

Like most of our writers, he has tried to ignore the fact that the theory of relativity applies in full to the universe of fiction; that there is no more place for a privileged observer in a real novel than in the world of Einstein. . . . M. Mauriac has put himself first. He has chosen divine omniscience and omnipotence. But novels are written *by* men and *for* men. In the eyes of God, who cuts through appearances and goes beyond them, there is no novel, no art; for art thrives on appearances. God is not an artist. Neither is M. Mauriac.[13]

Some of Sartre's objections to Mauriac and his Christian theory of predestination are equally relevant to the naturalistic novelists who believe in psychological determinism. In his essay *Qu'est-ce que la littérature?* Sartre specifically attacks these novelists, and links their cult of psychological determinism with the rise of the bourgeoisie in the nineteenth century. Sartre's argument is that the relationship of the writer to the reader has changed with the changes in the class structure. In the seventeenth century and before, the writer exercised a definite profession, with its rules and customs and its rank in society. In the eighteenth century these social moulds were broken: then every book was a new invention, "a kind of decision by the author regarding the nature of literature." The public was divided into two, and the writer had to satisfy contradictory demands; but Sartre believes that this state of tension was altogether healthy for the writer. Unfortunately, the golden age did not last, for the nineteenth century witnessed the rise of the bourgeoisie, and this meant that the best writers had no public, were indeed *against* the public that existed. This was because the rising bourgeoisie sought to dominate, and in effect to assimilate literature to the service of its needs. The bourgeoisie wanted only that kind of art which incorporated its own kind of psychology.

Sartre admits that in the seventeenth century literature had been, in a sense, reduced to psychology, but the psychology of Corneille and its contemporaries was "a cathartic appeal to freedom." Nineteenth-century psychology denied freedom. The capitalist rulers of that century wished it so; for the merchant, in the nature of his competitive and acquisitive calling, "distrusted the freedom of the people he dealt with"; he only wanted "infallible recipes" for winning people over and dominating them:

Man had to be governable as a matter of course and by

modest means. In short, the laws of the heart had to be rigorous and without exceptions. The bourgeois bigwig no more believed in human freedom than the scientist believes in a miracle. And as his ethics were utilitarian, the chief motive of psychology was self-interest. For the writer it was no longer a matter of addressing his work as an appeal to absolute freedoms, but of exhibiting the psychological laws which determined him to readers who were likewise determined.

Idealism, psychologism, determinism, utilitarianism, the spirit of seriousness—that is what the bourgeois writer had to reflect to his public first of all. He was no longer asked to restore the strangeness and opacity of the world, but to dissolve it into elementary subjective impressions which made it easier to digest. . . .[14]

The point Sartre is making here is an original one. Marx and many other Left-wing critics of the bourgeoisie *themselves* uphold determinism. It is a central tenet of Marxism that the only way to control the world is to understand its deterministic nature. Sartre is an exceptional theorist of the Left in rejecting determinism as a bourgeois philosophy. Admittedly, the bourgeois theorists Sartre attacks are psychological determinists, whereas the Marxists are economic determinists; but this is incidental; Sartre's argument is directed against *any* theory which denies human freedom. His contention is that human freedom is a necessary condition of at least some forms of art, and certainly of imaginative literature. It is far from his intention to suggest, however, that human freedom can be taken lightly, or for granted. It is one of the points most stressed throughout Sartre's work that freedom is a *burden* on mankind, something to be borne with courage, at times with actual heroism. This thought receives its fullest elaboration in Sartre's first play, *Les Mouches*.

REFERENCES

1. *Q.L.*, p. 327 (228).
2. *Q.L.*, p. 251 (164).
3. *Q.L.*, p. 254 (167).
4. *Situations III*, p. 11.
5. *F.A.*, p. 55.
6. *Le Mur*, p. 27 (*Intimacy*, tr. Ll. Alexander, p. 66).
7. *Théâtre*, p. 102.
8. *Situations I*, pp. 36–57 (*L.P.E.*, pp. 7–23).
9. *Ibid.* p. 37 (7)
10. *Ibid.* p. 50 (18)
11. *Ibid.* p. 52 (20)
12. *Ibid.* p. 47 (14)
13. *Ibid.* p. 59 (23)
14. *Q.L.*, p. 160–1 (87).

CHAPTER IV

LES MOUCHES

Les Mouches is a revised version of an ancient Greek myth. Although other French dramatists, such as Giraudoux, Anouilh, and Gide, have pleased twentieth-century audiences with the same formula of mock antique, *Les Mouches* has been the least popular of Sartre's plays, despite the added prestige of its open interdiction by the Nazis in 1943. I believe it nevertheless to be one of his best works; its relative failure with the theatre-going public—a public which Sartre himself heartily despises[1] —is probably due to the fact that the text is so concentrated, the ideas so original, and the dialectic so intricate. The actual moral of the play is also somewhat ambiguous.

The legend is that of Orestes in Argos. In Sartre's version of the play, Orestes comes back to Argos in company with his tutor, to find the city where his father was once King plagued with flies and the people weighed down with guilt. Both his tutor and a stranger (who is Jupiter in disguise) try to hurry him away, but Orestes is determined to stay, feeling that the city is his own, and that he must do something, no matter what, to make himself once more belong to it. Aegisthus, who has killed Orestes' father, his own brother Agamemnon, and married Clytemnestra, Agamemnon's widow and mother of Orestes, is ruling the city in a knowledge of guilt. Remorse and a consciousness of sin binds the throne to the people, for the religion of the state is a religion of mortification and repentance. There is just one heretic, Electra, daughter of Clytemnestra and brother of Orestes. Kept in servitude by her mother and stepfather, Electra tries to

tell the Argive people on a day of national repentance
that their religion is false, that the Gods wish them only
to be happy. Jupiter, alarmed by this seditious outburst,
throws down a column of the temple, and turns the people
against Electra.

But Electra has by this time met Orestes. She had
always dreamed that one day her brother would return
and avenge the murder of her father. Orestes reveals his
identity to her, and promises that her dream will come
true. Jupiter again sends signs commanding Orestes to
leave Argos, but Orestes ignores them. Jupiter then warns
Aegisthus that Orestes means to kill him. When Aegisthus
asks Jupiter why he, as a God, does not prevent this
happening, Jupiter answers by revealing a secret: since
men have freedom, even a God cannot compel them.
Orestes overhears this, and goes forward with his plans:
he kills first Aegisthus, then his mother. Electra is so
shocked by the deed she had always hoped for that when
Jupiter appears and urges her to repent, she succumbs to
his pressure and does so.

Orestes, on the other hand, holds out. He asserts the
autonomy of his own morality and his own being against
the pretence of Jupiter that the universe belongs to the
Gods. Orestes accepts the responsibility for what he has
done, but he will accept no guilt, because he does not
believe that what he has done is wrong. So Orestes leaves
Argos with his head high.

The crucial scene of the play is that between Orestes
and Jupiter in the last act. Jupiter has reduced Electra to
tears of remorse, and is trying to win Orestes round. He
offers him the throne of Argos if he will repent. Orestes
replies that the offer disgusts him. Jupiter noticing
Orestes' proud posture, suggests that he has nothing to be
proud of, since he is "the most cowardly of murderers."
Orestes answers: "The most cowardly of murderers is the
one who feels remorse." At this point Jupiter puts on his
most grandiloquent voice and reminds Orestes that the

whole universe moves according to the law of the Gods, and he begs him to come back to nature and obedience. Orestes answers: "You are the King of the Gods, Jupiter, the King of the Stones and the Stars, the King of the Seas. But you are not the King of Men." Jupiter demands: "Have I not created you?" Orestes agrees, but adds that Jupiter has created him a free man. And as soon as he had been created a free being, man ceased to belong to the Gods. "I *am* my liberty," Orestes says.

Jupiter asks Orestes if he realises that in asserting his independence he is going away from the safety and happiness of the fold. To be free is to be an exile, to live in anguish. Orestes agrees. He knows that he is condemned—condemned to have no law but his own. He must find his own way of life, as every man must. "You are a God and I am free. We are equally alone, and our anguish is the same." Jupiter reminds Orestes of the suffering that must come in the wake of such a discovery, but Orestes tells him proudly: "Men are free, and human life begins on the other side of despair."[2]

Jupiter is a key figure of this play—Jupiter seen as, effectively, a monotheistic deity; in other words, as God. It might be thought strange that any avowed atheist should give such an important place to God; but Sartre's atheism is strange. He does not say with the conventional humanist that no significance can be ascribed to the word "God"; he does not brush the concept of God aside as an anachronistic fiction. What he calls the "Death" of God is for Sartre a matter of profound, even tragic significance. Although he ceased, we are told,[3] at the age of eleven to believe in the existence of God, he has retained what can only be described as a religious cast of mind. In a lecture he gave to the Club Maintenant in Paris in 1945, Sartre said:

The existentialist is strongly opposed to a certain type of secular moralism which seeks to suppress God at the least possible expense. Towards 1880, when the French professors endeavoured to formulate a secular morality, they said something like this—"God is a useless and costly hypothesis; so we will do without it. However, if we are to have morality, a society and a law-abiding world, it is essential that certain values should be taken seriously; they must have an *à priori* existence ascribed to them. It must be considered obligatory *à priori* to be honest, not to lie, not to beat one's wife, to bring up children and so forth . . . although, of course, there is no God." In other words—and this is, I believe, the purport of all that we in France call radicalism— nothing will be changed if God does not exist; we shall rediscover the same norms of honesty, progress, and humanity, and we shall have disposed of God as an out-of-date hypothesis which will die away quietly of itself. The existentialist, on the contrary, finds it extremely embarrassing that God does not exist, for there disappears with Him all possibility of finding values in an intelligible heaven. There can no longer be any good *à priori*, since there is no infinite and perfect consciousness to think it. . . . Dostoevsky once wrote "If God did not exist, everything would be permitted"; and that for existentialism is the starting-point.[4]

Unfortunately, this "starting-point" of existentialism is a mistake. It is not true that moral values depend logically on the existence of God. Ethics is not derived from theological postulates. On the contrary, as Leibniz pointed out, ethics is logically prior to theology. If we did not already have a conception of goodness we could not recognise the excellence of God, indeed we could not recognise God as God, for it is the nature of God to be all-good, all-wise, all-knowing, all-loving, and none of these moral attributes, by which God is defined, would be intelligible to a mind that did not already understand the moral concepts of goodness, wisdom, and love. If there were no moral values, we could not speak of God.

It is a vulgar and unphilosophical error to reverse this truth, and say that without God "everything is permitted," as if God could rationally be said to be the fount and origin of moral values. What can truly be said is that the conventional moral codes of many societies derive *historically* from religious systems. But historical derivation is very different from logical derivation. The problem of the nineteenth-century Radicals whom Sartre mentions was largely a practical or social one. A great many people in Europe had learned the habits of good conduct in response to a training in obedience to God-given commands. If the myth of God was removed, there might thus seem to be a danger of such people ceasing to behave well.

But is all this anxiety well founded? Is there really any evidence for thinking that people brought up in the Christian religion, and then losing this faith in God's existence, would tend to cease believing in serious moral principles, such as its being wrong to injure one's neighbour? I myself should expect them to cease believing only in ritualistic taboos, such as its being wrong to desecrate the Sabbath or to carve graven images. But here I betray myself as having a very different point of view from Sartre who takes so seriously the claim of Dostoevsky that "if God did not exist everything would be permitted."

Dostoevsky himself would not have said this if he had not been a Christian. He said it believing deeply that God *did* exist. As said by Dostoevsky the remark has special meaning. And it may well have been true, of Dostoevsky personally, that if he had not his belief in God to fortify him, he would have given way to his lustful and destructive impulses. At any rate Dostoevsky *felt* this; so the statement about everything being permitted if God did not exist can be read as something which states, not a general truth of philosophy, but one psychological fact, a feeling that Dostoevsky has about himself.

If Sartre has a similar feeling, this is part of what I

meant when I spoke of his *religious* temperament. He finds so much inspiration in Christian writers such as Dostoevsky and Kierkegaard because his feelings are so akin to theirs, and at the same time, so acutely alien to those of the great majority of humanists. I have said of *La Nausée* that Sartre dramatises, and exaggerates, the insecurity and unpredictability of experience in a universe where the laws of nature are not absolute laws. A corresponding criticism may be made of *Les Mouches*. Sartre dramatises and exaggerates the forlornness and abandonment of man in a world where there is no God-given moral law.

Nevertheless, Sartre makes some points in *Les Mouches* which are important and true, and not always seen to be true. Moral principles are not laid down by God, and they are not to be discerned in some mysterious realm of value. Men find or create their own moral values for themselves. Moral codes are based on man-made *decisions*, not on metaphysical intuitions. Furthermore, Sartre is entirely right, I believe, in the importance he ascribes to human freedom. To say that men have freedom is to say (among other things) that they are not the toys of the Gods, or any other power outside themselves. They are absolutely free, loose, independent, disconnected, isolated, "on their own." The future is entirely open. If there were a God who ordered everything, or even a God who *knew* everything, the future would have to be as God foresees it. Thus the non-existence of an omniscient omnipotent deity is one logically necessary condition of man's full liberty.

What I believe to be the central moral of *Les Mouches* is echoed by Sartre in one of his essays, where he writes: "Human freedom is a curse; but that curse is the unique source of the nobility of man."[5] But *Les Mouches* also poses certain moral problems which are left unanswered. We have noted Sartre's version of the legend: Orestes, in obedience to the ethos of vengeance, kills the murdering

usurper and his treacherous mother; in the end he leaves
Argos. How far can Sartre be thought to be upholding
the rightness of vengeance, the rightness of what is, after
all, a *feudal* ethos, the ethos, at best, of *El Cid*, the ethos
which Hamlet has such hesitation in following?

One answer to this question may be that *Les Mouches*
should be read as a Resistance play. From this point of
view we should not only note the resemblance between
the religion of national repentance in Sartre's Argos and
the religion of national repentance in Vichy France; we
should also take Aegisthus as a symbol of the German
usurper and Clytemnestra as a symbol of the French collaborators. Thus, in so far as the author upholds Orestes'
action of killing the usurper king and his own unfaithful
mother against the established moral tenets of religion
and society, he could be said to be upholding the action of
those French Resistance terrorists and saboteurs who
killed not only the German invader but their fellow
Frenchmen, against the moral tenets of the Catholic
hierarchy and the Pétainist state.

All this (although the Nazis did not see it until their
French collaborators pointed it out to them) might seem
plain enough. Even so, *Les Mouches* cannot altogether
satisfy the demands of those who would read it as a
Resistance play. The acts of assassination are, assuredly,
justified, but to what do they lead? Orestes, having killed
the King and Queen, simply leaves Argos. He does not
stay to contribute anything to the better government or
welfare of the city; he quits. The political murders have
simply been the assertion of *his own* moral autonomy, of
his own freedom; steps, perhaps, towards his own salvation.
They are, so to speak, private acts, not political acts at all.
Sartre's critic Francis Jeanson was so dissatisfied with the
ending of this play that he questioned the author about it
and recalls the conversation in his book *Sartre par lui-même*:

Sartre pointed out to me that the great theme of the

Resisters (non-Communist) was this: "We are fighting
the Germans, but that does not give us any right over
the period which will follow the War." Besides, writing
under the Occupation, a play which exalted the attitude of the Resistance, he had had to turn to an ancient
myth to ensure an adequate transposition for his theme.
But Sartre added at the same time: "It was obviously
not by chance that I chose *that* myth, and I could
easily, in choosing it, have invented another ending:
Orestes might, for example, have stayed among the
people of Argos in the role of an ordinary citizen,
working with them to establish a decent political
order."

If Sartre did not do this [Jeanson continues]; if he
chose to bring down the curtain on that noble and
distant posture of Orestes, might that not be because
the Resistance appeared to him in the first place as the
personal adventure of each Resistant, as a test of freedom which envisaged as yet no other response beside a
sort of *heroism of conscience*? I know that Sartre spoke as
early as 1944 of the "total responsibility" and the "historic role" of each man at the very heart of his "total
solitude," of that absolute "abandonment" to which
the soldiers of the underground army found themselves condemned. But if Orestes had really killed the
usurper and his accomplice from a concern for his
historic responsibilities, how is one to describe his
withdrawal—his treason—when he chooses to run away
from the very situation which he has himself created,
to wash his hands of it?[6]

Jeanson here, I think, is making a valid point. For
Orestes cannot well be regarded as a political hero when he
has no perceptible social conscience. Orestes asserts what
would generally be called the "freedom of the will"
(though Sartre eschews both the word "will" and the
faculty it designates) but Orestes does not assert any

principle of political freedom or social freedom. Nor, in bearing witness to the autonomy of morals does he affirm any systematic moral code. This is an even graver weakness.

Sartre tells us that every man must make his own moral code; but he leaves us with no means of judging between one morality and another. Indeed it looks much as if Sartre is saying in these early works that there is no judging between one morality and another. Roquentin found salvation in art; Orestes finds salvation in an act prompted by the primitive moral code of vengeance. How many other ways of salvation, how many other moralities, might there not be? As many as there are individual men?

One may recall in this connexion Simone de Beauvoir's first novel *L'Invitée*, another consciously existentialist work (written about the same time as *La Nausée*). In this novel, the older of the two women protagonists, Françoise, murders the younger, Xavière, and the last paragraph reads:

No one could condemn her or absolve her. Her act belonged to no one but herself. "It is I who desire it." It was her own will which had been accomplished; there was nothing now that divided her from herself. At last she had chosen. She had chosen herself.[7]

Simone de Beauvoir explains in her memoirs that she came in time to feel dissatisfied with this ending of her novel, on the grounds that "an act of murder is no solution to the complex problem of personal relations." However, as the book stands, its moral reasoning is precisely that which Sartre deploys in *Les Mouches*. Orestes and Françoise invoke the same plea. They have acted in obedience to their own choice; there is no judging them because there is no universal moral law by which to judge them. But Sartre in fact has more to say than this.

Sartre's argument is that, since every man creates his own values, there is no "higher" standard by which to appraise one man's moral values in relation to another. But this is not to say that Sartre has no "objective" standard. He offers us the criterion of *sincerity*, genuineness or authenticity. The word "sincerity" is not itself very prominent in his writings, but what does recur again and again is an expression which is its opposite: *mauvaise foi*, which may be variously translated into English as "bad faith," "self-deception," "insincerity." What Sartre is saying is that since men are free, autonomous moral beings, creators of their own values, the one thing we can ask of them is that they should be true to their own values. For indeed if they are not true to those values, those values are not *real* values at all; they are just words. It is only in action that a man shows us what his morals are. Sincerity is therefore all-important.

This can be seen to be connected with Sartre's rejection of "essentialism." An "essentialist" can speak of a man who has a good nature but who behaves badly. An existentialist cannot. The goodness of a man's "nature" is the goodness of his behaviour. In existentialist eyes, what a man *is* is the sum total of what he *does*. It would be an absurdity for the existentialist to say that a man who acts badly is "essentially" good. There is no invisible essence to *be* good.

REFERENCES

1. See Sartre's interview with K. P. Tynan, *Observer* (London), 18 Jun. 1961.
2. *Théâtre*, p. 102.
3. *S.L.*, p. 173.
4. *E.H.*, p. 33.
5. *S.L.*, p. 157.
6. *S.L.*, pp. 150–1.
7. Quoted in Cranston, "Simone de Beauvoir," *London Magazine*, (May, 1954), p. 67.

CHAPTER V

L'ETRE ET LE NÉANT

The time has now come to turn to Sartre's purely philosophical works, and in particular to *L'Etre et le néant*. Although this is a highly technical book, it is no less dramatic than his literary writings. People generally expect philosophers to be calm, measured, unemotional writers. Sartre is the very reverse of this; he expresses his ideas in colourful language and startling aphorisms. The colour is sometimes so dazzling that it becomes blinding.

Let us first consider, then: What does it mean to be an existentialist? Sartre himself gives the simplest answer to this question in his lecture of 1945 to the Club Maintenant *L'Existentialisme est un humanisme*, where he explains that what all existentialists have in common is their belief "that *existence* comes before *essence*." He elaborates the point in these words:

If one considers an article of manufacture—as, for example, a book or a paper-knife—one sees that it has been made by an artisan who had a conception of it; and [that] he has paid attention, equally, to the conception of a paper-knife and to the pre-existent technique of production which is a part of that conception. . . .[1]

For this reason, Sartre continues, one can say of a paper-knife that its essence precedes its existence. Likewise in the minds of those who have visualised God, the Creator, as a "supernatural artisan," the "conception of man in the mind of God is comparable to that of a paper-knife in the mind of the artisan." Sartre then remarks how the "philosophic atheists of the eighteenth

D

century" rejected the notion of God, while retaining the idea that man's essence preceded his existence. Sartre claims that his own kind of atheistic existentialism is more consistent in holding that "if God does not exist, there is at least one being whose existence comes before its essence, a being which exists before it can be defined by any conception of it." That being is man.

Sartre goes on to explain further what he means by saying that existence precedes essence:

We mean that man first of all exists, encounters himself, surges up in the world—and defines himself afterwards. If man as the existentialist sees him is not definable, it is because to begin with he is nothing. He will not be anything until later, and then he will be what he makes of himself. Thus there is no human nature, because there is no God to have a conception of it. Man simply is. Not that he is simply what he conceives himself to be, but he is what he wills, and as he conceives himself after already existing—as he wills to be after that leap towards existence. Man is nothing else but that which he makes of himself. That is the first principle of existentialism. And that is what people call its "subjectivity," using the word as a reproach against us. But what do we mean to say by this, but that man is of greater dignity than a stone or a table? For we mean to say that man primarily exists—that man is, before all else, something which propels itself towards a future and is aware that it is doing so. Man is, indeed, a project which possesses a subjective life, instead of being a kind of moss, or a fungus, or a cauliflower. Before that projection of the self nothing exists; not even the heaven of intelligence: man will only attain existence when he is what he purposes to be.[2]

I have quoted already (above, p. 6) a mildly impatient remark of Simone de Beauvoir's about Sartre's being "enamoured, as ever, of a synthesis." He is, indeed, far removed from the kind of philosopher who is concerned with the piecemeal analysis of particular problems. Sartre, like Hegel, is interested in philosophy as one total system, as a map of the universe and a theory of man's whole nature. And although he follows Kierkegaard in rejecting Hegel's method of depicting the universe in terms of abstract mind, and in making the individual's inner experience of existence the foundation of his metaphysics, Sartre is nevertheless intensely Hegelian in his passion for synthesis, in his attachment to the dialectic, and in his rationalism.

Sartre begins, as Descartes begins, with one proposition that seems indubitable: "I think, therefore I am." *Cogito, ergo sum.* But he immediately corrects it. The Cartesian *cogito*, he points out, is a form of reflexion on the state of one's own consciousness. Consciousness turns back on itself and regards its own activities. But this is not a proof that "I am." Consciousness *is*, and so, in another way, the object of which one is conscious *is*. Consciousness reveals the world; it does not directly reveal itself to itself. Thus Sartre departs from Descartes's position, and adopts the view put forward by Husserl that all consciousness is "intensional," or, in other words, that consciousness must always, of its nature, be directed towards some object. Just as a mirror has no content except that which is reflected in it, so consciousness can have no content except the objects on which it reflects. Yet such an object is always separate and distinct from the consciousness which "mirrors" it.

These views are already adumbrated in Sartre's pre-War works. In *L'Etre et le néant* they form the starting-point for an elaborate theory of ontology. The Sartrian *cogito* yields two sorts of beings: consciousnesses and objects of consciousness. These two entities exist in different ways. Sartre says that a consciousness has being for-itself (*pour-soi*). The object on which consciousness reflects has being in-itself (*en-soi*). This distinction, at first rather odd-looking, soon becomes fairly easy to manipulate. The in-itself has objective being. It exists. It can be looked at, touched, heard, smelt, or tasted. In a word, it can be perceived. But what about that entity which does the perceiving? It is not itself a perceptible object, and yet it has being of a kind, as Sartre says, *for* itself. I have the experience of thinking about something. I am conscious of my own experience. But what is this "I"? Does it exist? Not as a table or chair exists; nor even as my body exists. Yet in a way I am my body, and my body is a being in-itself. Only this being in-itself, the object which I call my body, is separated from the "I" which is thinking about it. Separated: but what separates it, according to Sartre is something we can only speak of as "nothingness," or "le néant."

Of this nothingness Sartre has a great deal that is original, and surprising, to say. He requires us to acknowledge that whereas a being in-itself *is*, a being for-itself *is not*. Being in-itself is as it appears. There is no difference between appearance and reality. Being in-itself has no inside which is opposed to an outside.

But [and here I quote Professor Norman Greene] all cause, potency, particularity, purpose, and relationships with other objects, although appearing as structures of the object, are the result of the activity of the for-itself, *i.e.* are subjective in origin. The world as it appears to reflection is a combination of the objective characteristics of the in-itself—factual existence, solidity, quality and movement; and the subjective contribution of the perceiving for-itself—particularity, order, change, value and instrumentality.[3]

To these forms of being, Sartre adds a third (of which I shall have more to say later in this essay), namely being for-others. The consciousness, or for-itself, discovers that it has an objective existence as a human reality (Heidegger's expression) for other people. "If there is an

Other," Sartre writes, "... I have an outside. I have a nature."[4] We must remember, in this connexion, that, as for-itself, I am nothing. Hence the paradoxical conclusion that I am what I am not, and I am not what I am.

Man is not what he is, since he transcends his past by not being it in the present. At the same time, man is what he is not, in the sense of being an undetermined future, which he is not in the present. The present is the nothingness of pure existence, and only takes on meaning in the light of the dead past or prospective future behaviour.[5]

Precisely because of the void which divides the for-itself from the in-itself, a man cannot *be* in a fixed and final manner: he has continuously to choose, to make decisions, to reaffirm old purposes and projects or to affirm new ones. He is continuously engaged on the task of self-construction, a task which is never completed, but only ended by his death. This is why Sartre says there is no such thing as human nature, but only a human condition:

What men have in common is not a nature, but a metaphysical condition; and by that we mean the combination of constraints which limit them *à priori*; the necessity to be born, and to die; that of being finite and of dwelling in a world among men. For the rest, they constitute indestructible totalities, whose ideas, moods and acts are secondary and dependent structures, and whose essential character is to be *situated*, and they differ among themselves as their situations differ.[6]

We must now take a closer look at Sartre's notion of non-being or nothingness or "le néant." In every kind of question, Sartre argues, we stand before a being which we are questioning. The question entails a kind of expectation; that is to say, the questioner expects a reply. And since that reply may be either a "yes" or a "no," in the very act of posing the question we face the objective existence of a non-being:

> There exists then for the questioner the permanent possibility of a negative reply. In relation to this possibility, the questioner, by the very fact that he is questioning, posits himself as in a state of indetermination; he *does not know* whether the reply will be affirmative or negative. Thus the question is a bridge set up between two non-beings: the non-being of knowing in man, the possibility of non-being of being in transcendant being. . . . We set out upon our pursuit of being, and it seemed to us that the series of our questions had led us to the heart of being. But behold at the moment when we thought we were arriving at this goal, a glance cast on the question has revealed to us suddenly that we are encompassed with nothingness.[7]

Sartre will not accept the Kantian view that the idea of nothing can be derived from negative judgments, for he maintains that we could have negative judgments without a prior conception of negation. He also resists the Hegelian notion that being and non-being have an equal ontological status. Being, he insists, must come first. Nothingness is derivative from being. It "haunts" being; in a memorable phrase, Sartre says: "Nothingness lies coiled in the heart of being, like a worm."

Dissenting from Kant and Hegel, he dissents equally from Heidegger's idea that "Nothing annihilates itself" (*Das Nicht nichtet*). He argues that nothingness can nihilate itself only against a background of being; more precisely, it does not nihilate itself, it *is* nihilated ("est néantisé"). From this it follows that there must exist in the world a being with the capacity to nihilate nothingness, and also to sustain nothingness in its being. Now this cannot be a being in-itself. It must, therefore, be the other form of being—the for-itself, consciousness. "Man,"

Sartre concludes, "is the being through which nothingness comes into the world."

Sartre sees an intimate connexion between this principle of nothingness and the freedom of man. Nothing compels me to act one way rather than another; and because the future is open, nothingness confronts me as I look into the future. In face of this void I naturally feel dread or anguish. The same dread or anguish which reveals nothingness to me is the proof of my freedom. Consciousness moves all the time, and it sees itself continually as a nihilation of its own past being. The characteristic experience of consciousness is to choose: and to elect one possibility is to nihilate the possibilities we reject.

It is not easy to make up one's mind as to what is true or false in Sartre's theory of nothingness; and one may suspect that some of it at least is neither true nor false but simply meaningless. Professor A. J. Ayer, in the first appraisal of Sartre's philosophy to appear in English—a hostile, but brilliant analysis—dealt briskly with this problem:

... Sartre's reasoning on the subject of *le néant* seems to me exactly on a par with that of the King in *Alice through the Looking Glass*: "I see nobody on the road," said Alice. "I only wish I had such eyes," remarked the King. "To be able to see Nobody! And at that distance, too!" And again, if I remember rightly, "Nobody passed me on the road." "He couldn't have done that, or he would have been here first." In these cases the fallacy is easy enough to detect, but although Sartre's reasoning is less engagingly naïve, I do not think it is any better. The point is that words like "nothing" and "nobody" are not used as the names of something insubstantial and mysterious; they are not used to name anything at all. To say that two objects are separated by nothing is to say that they are *not* separated; and that is all that it amounts to. What Sartre does, however, is to say that being separated by Nothing, the objects are both united and divided. There is a thread between them; only it is a very peculiar thread, both invisible and intangible.'[8]

Ayer's criticism seems to me a pertinent one; but I think it may be answered. When Sartre talks of nothing-ness—and this is a fairer translation of *le néant* than "nothing"—he is introducing a quasi-technical term to do what Ayer says the word "nothing" does not ordinarily do, that is, to name "something insubstantial." Sartre sometimes uses "nothingness" to indicate mere negation; but the main purpose of the term is to name that *void*, or *emptiness* by which a being for-itself is encompassed, and divided from objects in-themselves.

Besides, when Sartre speaks of nothingness, his situation is not like that of the White King on the road with Alice, discussing the comings and goings of the messengers; it is that of someone who is acutely conscious of what is absent. The situation is rather closer to that of a widow returning from her husband's funeral and finding there is nobody in the house. The absence, the emptiness, is *felt*. Sartre himself gives the example of a man going into a café to meet his friend Pierre and noticing that Pierre is not there. When this man says "Pierre is not in the café" he is saying something very different, Sartre points out, from saying that "Wellington is not in the café." Both statements have an equal logical status; they are both true; but the signification is entirely different. Looking for Pierre, expecting to see him, and failing to do so, I become aware of a void:

> This does not mean that I discover his absence in some precise spot in the establishment. In fact Pierre is absent from the *whole* café; his absence fixes the café in its evanescence; the café remains *ground*; it persists in offering itself as undifferentiated totality to my only

marginal attention; it slips into the background; it pursues its nihilation. Only it makes itself ground for a determined figure; it carries the figure everywhere in front of it, presents the figure everywhere to me. This figure which slips constantly between my look and the solid real objects of the café is precisely a perpetual disappearance; it is Pierre raising himself as nothingness on the ground of the perpetual nihilation of the café.[9]

The experience of nothingness one has in looking in vain for a friend in a café is a relatively trivial experience. The experience of nothingness we have when we become aware of the void which divides us from the world of objective existence, i s a profoundly disturbing one. I have spoken of this in connexion with *La Nausée*. Sartre does not mean the diary of Antoine Roquentin to be read as an abnormal case history. Nausea and anguish, he believes, are part of the experience of us all. Nausea is the natural feeling that comes to anyone who confronts the fluid, sticky, viscous mess which constitutes the world of sensible appearance. Anguish is the natural feeling that comes from confronting the absolute openness of our own future, the nothingness in the centre of which we live.

Some readers may protest that they do not feel such nausea, or such anguish. Sartre has a short answer to them. People who say that they have no such feelings have run away from their nausea and anguish; they have protected themselves by *self-deception*. They have practised bad faith, or *mauvaise foi*. I do not myself find this notion of bad faith a convincing one, but I shall try to explain what Sartre means by it. Primarily it takes the form of persuading oneself that one is what one is not, or that one is doing what one is not doing. Sartre gives the example of a young woman going to a restaurant for the first time with an admirer who, in the course of the evening takes her hand. She pretends not to notice; she leaves her hand limply in his, her mind "preoccupied" with the higher things her admirer is talking about. Another of Sartre's examples is that of a café waiter, *acting his rôle*. We look at the waiter:

> His movement is quick and forward, a little too precise, a little too rapid. He comes towards the patrons with a step a little too quick. He bends forward a little too eagerly; his voice, his eyes express an interest a little too solicitous for the order of the customer. . . . All his behaviour seems to us a game. . . . But what is he playing? We need not watch long before we can explain it: he is playing at *being* a waiter in a café.[10]

Both the girl with the inert hand and the over-zealous waiter are *pretending* to themselves. They are assuming the rôle of entities with fixed and determined natures; they are running away from the reality of the responsible, free, and unpredictable for-itself into a false simulation of an object in-itself. Sartre believes that bad faith of this kind is much encouraged in the modern world by the teaching of Freud. He thinks that Freud offers people the means of escape from responsibility into the myth of being creatures determined by unconscious forces. Sartre's rejection of Freud's theory of the unconscious follows from his identification of "human reality" with consciousness. But he cannot neglect the psychological problems which led Freud to introduce the concept of the unconscious. Sartre simply says that those experiences which lie at the origin of neurosis and which Freud classifies as unconscious are, in reality, conscious. If they are forgotten, that it is not because they are kept from consciousness by the workings of a hidden censor; it is because men, in their bad faith, have put them out of their minds. As opposed to the Freudian notion of unconscious wishes unconsciously repressed, Sartre speaks much more harshly, of falsehood, of men denying what, if they are frank with themselves, they *know* what they want, or once wanted, to do.

The trouble, it seems to me, with this theory of bad

faith, is simply that there is no room for a discussion of its merits. It is part of the teaching of Freudian psychology that its findings will be resisted, so that any resistance to it is taken as confirmation of its truth. The same is even more true of Sartre's theory of bad faith. If a critic denies it, the denial will only be taken as evidence of the critic's own bad faith. Mrs Warnock makes this point well in an excellent and by no means unsympathetic essay on Sartre's ethics:

... suppose that one denied, as I think one very well might, that nausea was what one experienced when contemplating the external world. Suppose that, to be more specific still, one denied that the viscosity of things had any particular effect on one at all; suppose one said the suggestion that viscosity is an important category of the material was nothing but neurotic ... would not all these denials be taken simply as instances of bad faith? They probably would. If bad faith can be crudely defined as the refusal to face disagreeable facts, then one's denials can always be construed as such a refusal. And the more vigorous one's protests that this is not self-deception, that it is only to falsehoods or exaggerations that one is objecting, the more serious the accusation of bad faith would become.[11]

In fairness to Sartre one must at this point add that although the concept of bad faith is a weapon against which no defence would work, Sartre has never, to my knowledge, actually invoked it against anyone who has criticised him as certain disciples of Freud have invoked their concept of "resistance" against people who have criticised them.

REFERENCES

1. *E.H.*, p. 17 (26).
2. *E.H.*, p. 21 (28).
3. N. H. Greene, *Jean-Paul Sartre*, Ann Arbor 1960, p. 19.
4. *E.N.*, p. 321 (263).
5. Greene, *op. cit.*, pp. 25–26
6. *Situations II*, p. 22.
7. *E.N.*, p. 39 (5).
8. *Horizon*, (July 1945), pp. 18–19.
9. *E.N.*, p. 45 (10).
10. *E.N.*, pp. 98–9 (59).
11. Mary Warnock, *Ethics since 1900*, London 1960, p. 182.

CHAPTER VI

SARTRIAN PSYCHO-ANALYSIS

The time has now come to say more about **Sartre's third** form of being—being *for-others*; and about the manner in which he develops this notion, particularly in that section of *L'Etre et le néant* dealing with "concrete relations" between people. Sartre does not in general accept Berkeley's doctrine that "to exist is to be perceived," but he does adopt it, in a somewhat roundabout way, in the case of the existence of human beings. According to Sartre it is only in a very indirect and complicated way that I can be said to exist as an object for myself. But he believes that I exist in a direct and simple way as an object for other people. They see me as part of the furniture of their external world. They observe my behaviour. I, seeing them see me, and knowing that they observe my behaviour, acquire, through them, this added form of being which Sartre calls being "for-others."

Hegel also believed that our self-consciousness exists only because it exists for another person and that we must exist for others in order to exist for ourselves. Sartre might be quoting from Hegel when he says "the road of interiority passes through the Other." I am an object only because I exist as an object for another person; I need from the other person an acknowledgment of my being; he is the mediator between me and myself. All this is summed up in what Sartre calls the look or gaze. If I exist for another person, I do so through his look. The relationship is reciprocal. To another person I am in my turn the Other. My gaze gives him objective existence. And so "the value of the other's recognition of me depends on my recognition of the other."[1] Nor is this all. In so far as the look of another person turns me into an object, it turns me into something "solidified," something with a "character"; and so, in a sense, it takes away my freedom. Correspondingly my look at the other takes away, in the same sense, the freedom of him who becomes an object for me. Thus we are presented with a kind of metaphysical struggle or conflict of two "transcendences" each of which tries to out-transcend the other. As Professor Stern says:

> Of course, it is not precisely the eyes as physiological organs which look at me: it is the other person as a subject, a consciousness. The gaze of the other person includes all kinds of judgements and evaluations. Being seen by the other person means to grasp oneself as an unknown object of unrecognizable judgements. A judgement according to Sartre is the transcendental act of a free person. The fact of being seen changes me into a being without defences against a freedom which is not my freedom. Being seen by the other person makes us slaves; looking at the person, we are masters. I am a slave as long as I depend in my being on the freedom of another self, which is not mine but a condition of my being. And I am master, when I make the other self depend for its being on my freedom.[2]

Sartre does not shrink from these implications of his theory. On the contrary, he puts forward the extreme and grim opinion that all concrete relations between people are forms of conflict or struggle. He starts off by saying that it is the experience of *shame* which proves to us the existence of other people. Shame, he points out, is a form of recognition or acknowledgment. I should not feel shame if there was nobody else in the world to be a witness to my actions. In shame, I "recognise that I *am* as the Other sees me"; that is, "I am ashamed of myself as I *appear* to the Other."[3]

Elsewhere in the same chapter, Sartre writes:

If there is an Other, whatever or whoever he may be, whatever may be his relations with me, and without his acting upon me in any way, except by the pure upsurge of his being—then I have an outside. I have a *nature*. My original fall is the existence of the Other. Shame—like pride—is the apprehension of myself as a nature, although that very nature escapes me and is unknowable as such. Strictly speaking it is not that I lose my freedom in order to become a *thing*, but my nature is—over there, outside my lived freedom—as a given attribute of this being which I am for the Other.[4]

How do we behave in this situation? Sartre sees only two general lines of conduct open to us. We may either try to make ourself the sort of object in the eyes of the other that we wish to be. Or we may try to take away the other's freedom. Both are forms of conflict; the first finding its extreme expression in masochism, the second in sadism.

I may fancy I am well-mannered and honest. But I am well-mannered and honest, Sartre says, only because another person sees me thus. Yet I do not want to owe my being in this way to another: I want to claim it as my own. How can I succeed in this? I may think that I can do it if I absorb the other person's liberty, while still leaving that liberty free. This is attempted by what Sartre calls "seduction." If I can make the Other accept me as the supreme in-itself of his (or her) own existence, the Other's liberty is preserved and my own facticity is not jeopardised. At the same time, I do not wish to be so identified with myself that my own transcendence can never emerge. So I try to uphold my own subjectivity while the Other sees me as an object. As a seducer, posing as an object, I try to capture the other's subjectivity. I make myself a fascinating object; I use fascinating language. However, Sartre goes on to say, language is a device which is incapable of realising such ends. For language needs to be *understood*. That is to say, language is something which the Other must interpret in his own freedom, his own transcendence. Thus language can never take away that very faculty which is needed for language itself to function.

It is for these reasons that Sartre describes love as a project which can never be realised. For me to love you is, in Sartre's view, nothing other than my trying to make you love me. And, since for you to love me is simply for you to try to make me love you, we are each confronted by an infinite regress. We may engage in prolonged essays in mutual seduction, but we are doomed to an eternal frustration. Moreover, Sartre adds that even if two lovers could sustain for a lifetime a relationship of perpetual tension, the presence of a third person in the world would ruin their enterprise. For the look or gaze of this other person is enough to bring about the "petrification of their love-relationship in a dead possibility."

Because love is an impossible enterprise, one may turn to the more desperate endeavour of masochism. But this again, Sartre says, cannot achieve its end. Masochism is an assumption of guilt. I am guilty towards myself since I consent to my absolute alienation. I am guilty towards the Other, since I furnish him with the occasion to be guilty. "Masochism is an attempt not to fascinate the other by means of my objectivity, but to cause myself to be fascinated by my objectivity-for-others."[5] Even so, masochism is, and must be, a failure. For the more the masochist tries to taste his objectivity, the more does he become submerged by the consciousness of his subjectivity. Even the man who pays a woman to whip him is treating her as an instrument.

Sartre brackets love and masochism together since they are both attempts to assimilate the liberty of the Other, while allowing it to remain free. But there are other types of relationship based on the desire to transform the

Other, to objectify him. One may perhaps try *indifference*. This is a kind of "blindness" towards others, or, more exactly, a deliberate refusal to accept the fact that others are looking at me. Thus it is a form of bad faith. And it can be sustained as long as my bad faith desires. There are men, Sartre says, who live and die without ever having "suspected what the Other is."[6] But he adds that even if one is entirely immersed in this state of indifference, one does not cease to experience its inadequacy. And, as in the case of all bad faith, it is the condition itself which furnishes one with the motive for ending it. For the Other as freedom, and my objectivity as my alienated self, are indubitably *there*. Hence a perpetual feeling of lack and uneasiness in the one who shuts his eyes. Without the Other, I face alone the terrible necessity of being free. I cannot put the responsibility for making myself *be* on to anyone but myself. I am a *for-itself* in a perpetual solitary pursuit of the *in-itself*. Moreover, if I am "blind," I can be seen without seeing. I become conscious of a wandering, an inapprehensible look; and I am in danger of its alienating me behind my back.

This uneasiness may prompt another attempt to get possession of the Other's freedom. If so, I shall pass from indifference to *desire*. This is to turn upon the Other, "and utilise him as an instrument in order to touch his freedom." This desire Sartre describes as "sexual." Against the view that sexuality is a contingent factor connected with our bodies, Sartre maintains that sexuality is a "necessary structure of being." He denies that sexual desire is a wish for pleasure; for desire, he points out, has a transcendent object. It is not just desire for a body, it is desire for the consciousness which gives meaning and unity to that body.

Desire itself is consciousness: "*I am* the one who desires and desire is a particular mode of my subjectivity."[7] At the same time, sexual desire is not a clear and distinct desire, comparable to the other appetites. Sartre writes:

E

We all know the famous saying "Make love to a pretty woman when you want her, just as you would drink a glass of cold water when you are thirsty." We all know how unsatisfactory and even shocking this statement is to the mind. This is because, when we do desire a woman, we do not keep ourselves wholly outside the desire. The desire *compromises* me; I am the accomplice of my desire. Or, rather, the desire has fallen wholly into complicity with the body. Let any man consult his own experience; he knows how consciousness is clogged, so to speak, by sexual desire; it seems that one is invaded by facticity; that one ceases to flee it and that one slides towards a *passive* consent to the desire. At other moments it seems that facticity invades consciousness in its very flight and renders consciousness opaque to itself. It is like a yeasty tumescence of *fact*.[8]

Desire, he goes on to say, is consent to desire. What is more, desire is not only the revelation of the Other's body, it is the revelation of my own body to myself. The *for-itself*, in Sartre's words, "experiences the vertigo of its own body." And the final stage of sexual desire can be a "swooning" which it is itself the final stage of "consent to the body." Desire is an appetite directed towards the Other, and it is lived as a consciousness making itself body. In desire "I make myself flesh in the presence of the Other in order to appropriate the Other's flesh." In Sartre's words, "I make myself flesh in order to impel the Other to realise *for herself* and *for me* her own flesh, and my caresses cause my flesh to be born for me, in so far as it is for the Other, flesh causing her to be born as flesh." This Sartre calls a "double reciprocal incarnation" which is the aim of desire: the "incarnation of consciousnesness in order to realise the incarnation of the Other."[9]

This leads him to put a further question. Why does consciousness nihilate itself in the form of desire? Partly, he says, it is because in my experience of desire I discover something like a "flesh" of object. But desire is not primarily a relation to the world; for in desire the world appears only as the background of the Other:

> Desire is an attitude aiming at enchantment. Since I can grasp the Other only in his* objective facticity, the problem is to ensnare his freedom within this facticity. It is necessary that he be "caught" in it as the cream is caught up by a person skimming milk. So the Other's for-itself must come to play on the surface of his body, and be extended all through his body; and by touching this body I should finally touch the Other's free subjectivity. This is the true meaning of the word *possession*. It is certain that I want to possess the Other's body, but I want to possess it only in so far as it is itself "possessed", that is, in so far as the Other's consciousness is identified with his body.[10]

Such in Sartrian psychology, is desire; and desire again (like love and masochism and indifference) is doomed to failure. For in the very satisfaction of desire pleasure arises, and pleasure "is the death of desire," its death, not only because it is the fulfilment of desire, but because it is its limit and its end. Nor is this all. In sexual relations, caressing is followed by acts of seizing and penetration. In the process, says Sartre, the Other ceases to be an incarnation; she† becomes once more an instrument. "Her consciousness, which played on the surface of her flesh, disappears under my sight; she remains no more than an *object*, with object images inside her." This does not mean that I cease to desire, but the desire has lost its goal. I feel this, and I suffer from a frustration I cannot precisely name. "I take and discover

---

* One may read the word "her" instead of "his." In the original French, where the gender of the noun rather than the sex of the person governs the pronoun, this choice is left open to the reader.

† Alternatively "he." (See note above.)

myself in the process of taking, but what I take in my hands is *something else* than what I wanted to take."[11] It is this situation which is the origin of sadism.

In sadism, as in desire, the goal is to seize and make use of the Other not only as object, but as a pure incarnated transcendence. The sadist emphasises the instrumental appropriation of the incarnated Other. He seeks to incarnate the other through violence. But, Sartre adds, sadism wants sexual relations to be non-reciprocal. It enjoys being a free appropriating power confronting a freedom captured by flesh. It is not the body for its own sake that the sadist seeks to master, but the Other's freedom. It is this enterprise which Sartre says is absurd. The sadist does not seek to *suppress* the freedom of the one whom he tortures "but to force this freedom freely to identify itself with the tortured flesh."[12] In fact, no matter what pressure is exerted on the victim, the abjuration remains *free*.

This is why sadism also is doomed to failure. The freedom the sadist seeks to appropriate is out of reach. And the more the sadist treats the Other as an instrument the more the freedom of the Other escapes him. The sadist discovers his error when his victim *looks* at him. For then the sadist experiences the absolute alienation of his being in the Other's freedom.

Sartre turns next to another, related form of relations with other people—hatred. The aim of hate, he says, is extinction of the Other; but this again is an aim that cannot be realised. For although I can kill a man, terminate his life, I *cannot bring it about that he had never existed*. I cannot realise his non-being. So hate, too, is doomed to permanent frustration.

What are we to make of this depressing catalogue of possible relations between people? Sartre does not claim to have given an exhaustive list of relationships, but he does maintain, first, that those which he has named are fundamental, and secondly, that all our complex patterns of conduct toward one are "enrichments" of these two original attitudes. Sartre insists that we can never hold a consistent attitude towards the Other, unless the Other is simultaneously revealed to us both as subject and as object, as transcendence-transcending and as transcendence-transcended, which is in principle impossible. "Thus, ceaselessly tossed from being-a-look to being-looked-at, falling from one to the other in alternate revolutions, we are always, no matter what attitude we adopt, in a state of instability in relation to the Other." Thus we meet each other as "competing transcendences"; and we shall never place ourselves concretely, Sartre says, on a plane of equality where "the recognition of the Other's freedom would involve the Other's recognition of our own freedom."[13]

This conclusion of *L'Etre et le néant* is not only a melancholy one: it is also sharply at variance with views Sartre has put forward elsewhere. For this reason it is important there should be no misunderstanding. There need be none, for Sartre's words are unambiguous:

The Other is on principle inapprehensible; he flees me when I seek him and possesses me when I flee him. Even if I should want to act according to the precepts of the Kantian morality, and take the Other's freedom as an unconditioned end, still this freedom would become a transcendence-transcended by the mere fact that I make it my goal. On the other hand, I could act for his benefit only by utilising the Other-as-object as an instrument in order to realise this freedom. . . . Thus I am brought to that paradox which is the perilous reef of all liberal politics and which Rousseau has defined in a single word: I must "force" the Other to be free. Even if this force is not always nor even very frequently exercised in the form of violence, nevertheless it still governs the relations of men with each other.[14]

Indeed Sartre goes on to say that from the moment I exist I establish a factual limit to the Other's freedom. Even tolerance, charity or *laissez faire*, is a project which engages me and engages the Other in his acquiescence. To be tolerant towards the Other, he says, is to cause the Other to be "thrown into a tolerant world" and, at the same time, to remove the Other "from those possibilities of courageous resistance, of perseverance, of self-assertion which he would have the opportunity to develop in a world of intolerance." Sartre then says that *"respect for the Other's freedom is an empty word"* [my italics], for "even if we could assume the project of respecting his freedom, each attitude which we adopted with respect to the Other would be a violation of that freedom which we claimed to respect."[15]

Sartre looks at the idea that there are some concrete experiences in which we discover ourselves not at odds with others, but in community with them—the experience of *Mitsein* or "togetherness." Such feelings, however, Sartre dismisses as purely psychological or subjective. They reveal nothing about being as such. It is altogether useless, he concludes, for man to try to escape from his dilemma: "One must either transcend the Other, or allow oneself to be transcended by him. The essence of the relations between consciousnesses is not the *Mitsein*; it is conflict."[16]

REFERENCES

1. Alfred Stern, *Sartre: His Psychology and Psychoanalysis*, New York 1953, p. 93.
2. *Op. cit.*, p. 97.
3. *E.N.*, p. 267 (222).
4. *E.N.*, p. 321 (263).
5. *E.N.*, p. 447 (378).
6. *E.N.*, p. 450 (381).
7. *E.N.*, p. 455 (386).
8. *E.N.*, pp. 456–7 (388).
9. *E.N.*, p. 460 (391).
10. *E.N.*, p. 463 (394).
11. *E.N.*, p. 468 (398).
12. *E.N.*, p. 472 (403).
13. *E.N.*, p. 479 (408).
14. *E.N.*, p. 479–480 (408–9).
15. *E.N.*, p. 480 (409).
16. *E.N.*, p. 502 (429).

CHAPTER VII

HUIS CLOS AND *LES CHEMINS DE LA LIBERTÉ*

The views on "concrete relations between people" put forward in *L'Etre et le néant* are given dramatic and arresting formulation in Sartre's second play, *Huis clos*, first performed in Paris just after the Liberation in 1944. Despite the austerity of the notions that it contains, this has been one of his most successful plays with the theatre-going public, and has also been filmed.

As in *Les Mouches*, the author makes effective use in *Huis clos* of the myths of the religion he rejects. The play is set in Hell. But it is an unexpected kind of Hell. It takes the form of a room furnished, albeit sparsely, in the style of the Second Empire. There are no windows and no mirrors, but there are three sofas, one each for the three characters of the play—Garcin, Inès, and Estelle. They all know they have come to Hell, but each, entering the room in turn, is surprised to find none of the proverbial fires or instruments of torture. In the end they discover the truth: they are to be their own tormentors; each tortures the others.

Garcin and Estelle are both cowards and hypocrites; it is Inès who forces them to admit it. Garcin is the first to arrive, and when Inès is shown into the room, she asks him rudely why he is looking so frightened. He tells her coldly that he is not afraid, and suggests that since they are forced to be in each other's company, they should try to be polite. Inès, a brusque Lesbian, assures him that she is not a polite woman. Estelle, however, when she appears, shares with Garcin the wish to ease the tension of the situation by civilised behaviour. We suspect that if Inès were not there, these two would get on well together. They exchange lies about the circumstances which brought them to Hell. Garcin says that he is a pacifist who has been shot for his views; Estelle, who is young and pretty, says that she married a rich old man to get money for her family and then committed adultery with a man she loved.

Inès laughs at both their stories. How would either be damned, she asks, if he had been a hero and she a saint? Why not tell the truth? Garcin resists for a while; then agrees to confess. He has been cruel to his wife for five years; taken mistresses to his home, coloured women, and made his wife bring them breakfast in bed. "Cad," says Inès. "And you?" asks Garcin. Inès confesses that she persuaded a woman to leave her husband to live with her and then made the woman feel so guilty that she turned on the gas, killing both Inès and herself. Estelle then tells her story: she has driven her lover to suicide by killing their baby. "Well," observes Inès, "here we are, stripped naked."

Garcin proposes that they should try to help each other; but again Inès rebuffs him; she has no need of help. Estelle is friendlier; she is even ready to give herself to him. But Garcin is not content with the good opinion of Estelle; he wants the good opinion of Inès as well. He wants the good opinion of everybody. Then it comes out why he is damned; it is not for his cruelty to his wife, but for cowardice. He had tried to run away from the War, and had been caught, and died a coward's death. This is what worries him. His friends are thinking what a coward he is. He asks Estelle: "Do you love me?" Estelle replies: "Do you think I could love a coward?"

Garcin bangs on the door to be let out. But when the door opens he will not leave. He turns back to Inès. He cannot bring himself to go without having convinced her that he is not a coward. He asks her; "Is it possible to be a coward when one has chosen the most dangerous way of life? Can you judge a whole life by one act?" Inès says: "You dream of heroic deeds, but in the moment of danger, you run away." Garcin claims that he did not just dream of heroism; he chose it. Inès asks for proof. "It is deeds alone which show what a man has willed," she tells him. Garcin replies: "I died too soon. I did not have enough time to do *my* deeds." "One always dies too soon," Inès says, "or too late. And, now your life's finished. It's time to make up the account. You *are* nothing other than your life."

Garcin is furious with Inès; and Estelle, who has also come to hate her, suggests that he should take his revenge by making love to her, under the eyes of Inès. Garcin caresses Estelle, but he cannot escape the contemptuous gaze of Inès, and her voice crying "Coward, coward!" Estelle takes up a paper-knife and stabs Inès; but of course she cannot kill someone who is already dead. So the play ends, with the three of them realising that they are condemned to each other's company for all eternity. Garcin has already made the discovery: "Hell is other people."

Huis clos is one of those plays that come wonderfully to life on the stage. One does not need to be versed in Sartre' philosophy to respond to the drama and the atmosphere of the piece; a Christian upbringing would be a perfectly adequate preparation. Nevertheless the play can only be fully understood in the light of the theories expounded in *L'Etre et le néant*.

Several of these ideas are put in the mouth of Inès. It is not that she is represented as virtuous. She is damned, like the others. Her own conduct has been cruel, and she would have no right to condemn Garcin on that score. Nor would she wish to; for although she is charmless and rude, Inès is not a hypocrite. Her intelligence and her aggressive honesty make her a bitterly effective persecutor of Garcin; to have her think him a coward is for him the worst torment.

The opinion of Estelle does not matter to him because
she is entirely frivolous. She is so selfish that she seems
to have no moral sense at all. She explains the crime for
which she has been damned, throwing her baby into the
lake, by saying that she just "didn't want it." Her intelligence is not quite as minimal as her conscience, but her
reproaches, if she reproached Garcin, would not trouble
him. She tortures him simply by being there. She is
attractive; she provokes desire. She in turn desires
Garcin. And there is nothing Garcin can do to satisfy this
desire, because the gaze of Inès is on them all the time.
Here we have a striking illustration of the argument in
L'Etre de le néant, that even if two people could maintain a
perpetual "love-relationship" based on the mutual pursuit
of the impossible, the presence of a third person in the
world would ruin the enterprise.

Another point is made in the dialogue between Inès
and Garcin. Garcin, in his bad faith, invokes the falsehood (as Sartre sees it) of essentialism to support his
pretence that, although he has committed cowardly acts,
he has a brave character or essence or soul. It is the role
of Inès to teach him the painful existentialist message
that a man *is* what he *does,* and no more. Garcin has no
essence to be brave. He is a coward because his deeds are
cowardly. In this connexion we must not forget one point
about *Huis clos*—though it is one which Sartre's critics do
sometimes forget—and that is that all the characters are
dead. They are no longer free beings. Their lives are
terminated, and so, although they have no essences, they
do have complete biographies. Put in another way, they
have no future; and they can have no more projects.
They are thus damned in the sense that the possibility of
salvation is no longer open to them. If Garcin had been
alive, there would be a continuing possibility of his
ceasing to do cowardly deeds and starting to do brave
deeds, and thus of turning from a coward into a brave
man. But as he is dead, it is, as Inès tells him, *too late.* He

can no longer become a brave man. Death has closed the account.

Sartre's placing *Huis clos* in Hell is therefore no mere theatrical device. It is properly placed in Hell, because one of the central themes of the play is damnation. In this way, it explores the other side of the subject of salvation, which is also examined in *La Nausée* and *Les Mouches*. Damnation, one may imagine, is an easier subject than salvation to manipulate artistically. At all events, *Huis clos* is a small masterpiece of dramatic literature, a dense, rich, beautifully-constructed play which cries out to be acted, and which is particularly suited to the shut-in structure of the intellectual *théâtre de poche*. We shall not find the same merits in Sartre's next important work, *Les Chemins de la liberté*; for here we pass from the one-act play to the four-volume novel, from the closed tight claustrophobic world of the damned to the open, loose, agoraphobic world of the living; and we return once more to the theme of freedom and salvation. But we shall find that we do not escape from the grim philosophy of *L'Etre et le néant*.

Les Chemins de la liberté is a sort of tapestry, intended to give a synoptic picture of different people's "roads to freedom"; but it is woven in a variety of styles, and has been abandoned unfinished. The first and second volumes, *L'Age de raison* and *Le Sursis*, both appeared in 1945; the third volume, *La Mort dans l'âme*, came out in 1949, and in November and December of that same year Sartre published in his review *Les Temps modernes* two chapters, entitled "*Drôle d'Amitié*," of the projected last volume. Later Sartre announced that he intended to write no more of it.

The first volume, *L'Age de raison*, could easily stand as a novel on its own. It has a hero, Mathieu, whose concentrated experiences over a few days lead him from one set of illusions about freedom to another, equally foolish. The second volume, *Le Sursis*, is an altogether different kind of novel. Closely modelled on the American "realist" technique of John Dos Passos, it is an attempt to convey the history of Munich week in France by a *montage* of different people's reactions, cutting quickly, sometimes in the same sentence, from what is being said and thought by one person to what is being said and thought by another, and from fictional characters like Mathieu to real people, such as Chamberlian and Daladier. Thus we are with a vengeance "tossed," in the memorable phrase of *Qu'est-ce que la littérature?*, "from one consciousness to another." However, in his third volume, *La Mort dans l'âme*, the author returns to the more conventional technique of *L'Age de raison*, in order to concentrate once more on the fortunes of a small company of imaginary persons. The published fragments of the unfinished fourth volume are a continuation of the last section of *La Mort dans l'âme*.

I have called Mathieu the "hero" of the first book, but it would be a mistake to think of him as the one for whom Sartre has particular sympathy or admiration; still less should we think of him as any kind of autobiographical figure. Critics have done so; we find Professor Stern referring to "Mathieu-Sartre," and even Miss Murdoch says that Mathieu "is no doubt a portrait of Sartre himself." In truth there is considerably less of Sartre in Mathieu than there is in Roquentin. Mathieu is, admittedly, like Sartre, a professor of philosophy who becomes a soldier, if an altogether more belligerent one; but there is no real identity between them. Indeed there is a certain irony in the way in which Sartre makes this professor of philosophy one of the most self-deceiving of all his major characters.

As the novel opens Mathieu is told by his mistress Marcelle that she is pregnant, and he spends the next forty-eight hours trying to find the money to pay for the abortion. He is too scrupulous to let her go to a dirty old woman with a needle; he is equally resolute against the idea of marrying Marcelle so that she may have the baby. Although he feels old at thirty-four, Mathieu is firmly persuaded that marriage would jeopardise his liberty; for he fancies himself an extremely independent man. Marcelle says to him one day: "You want to be free, absolutely free. It's your vice." Mathieu is annoyed; he has explained his views on freedom to her a hundred times before, and she knows that it is what he has most at heart. But she tells him again: "It's your vice."

Mathieu hears of a refugee doctor who will perform the abortion for four thousand francs, and he goes to various people—his brother, his friends, and a money-lender's office—in a determined but unsuccessful attempt to borrow the money. By a nicely ironical touch, the author makes Mathieu's pompous bourgeois brother Jacques (an archetypal Sartrian "swine") the spokesman of some important truths. "If I had your ideas, I should be rather chary of asking favours of a damned bourgeois," Jacques tells Mathieu. "For I *am* a damned bourgeois. . . . And what is more, you, who despise the family, exploit our family ties to touch me for money." Mathieu tries to justify himself:

"Listen," said Mathieu, "there's a misunderstanding here: I care little whether I'm a bourgeois or whether I'm not. All I want is"—and he uttered the final words through clenched teeth and with a sort of shame— "to retain my freedom."

"I should have thought," said Jacques, "that freedom consisted in frankly confronting situations into which one had deliberately entered, and accepting all one's responsibilities. . . . You have, however, reached the age of reason, my poor Mathieu," said he in a tone of pity and of warning. "But you try to dodge that fact, too; you try to pretend that you are younger than you are. Well . . . perhaps I am doing you an injustice. Perhaps you haven't in fact reached the age of reason;

it's really a moral age . . . perhaps I've got there sooner than you have.[1]

As if to prove his brother's point, Mathieu consoles himself in the company of the very young. He has started going out with a White Russian girl of eighteen, Ivich, and her brother Boris, a kleptomaniac who was once one of his pupils. Ivich is still trying to pass her university entrance examination; Boris, an even more self-con- ciously youthful nineteen, is being pursued by Lola, an aging night-club singer. They go to a cabaret together, a somewhat pathetic quartet. Mathieu, eager to assert his liberty in the presence of Ivich, resorts to Gidean *actes gratuits*, that is, doing things for which he has no rational motive, such as ordering champagne, which he dislikes, and by sticking a knife into his own hand. Sartre well brings out the folly of such acts, and especially the folly of the Gidean idea that behaviour of this kind is in any way an assertion of freedom.

One morning Boris comes to Mathieu and Ivich, who are together in a café, and says that Lola has died while sleeping with him; he has fled in a panic, and is now anxious to recover the love-letters he has written to her. Mathieu volunteers to go for them. While he is searching Lola's cases, Mathieu comes upon some large bank notes. Here at last he sees a way of paying for Marcelle's abortion. But Mathieu hesitates so long that Lola, who is not dead, but in a drug addict's stupor, wakes up. Later, Mathieu has a new access of courage and goes back and steals the money.

In the meantime there have been developments. Mathieu's malicious homosexual friend Daniel has been seeing Marcelle and has persuaded her that she really wants to have the child. Thus when Mathieu appears at Marcelle's flat with the money for the abortion, Marcelle revolts against him and turns him out of the flat. Mathieu is presently informed that Daniel is going to marry

Marcelle. Daniel is ready to acknowledge Mathieu's child as his own. Homosexual as he may be, he assures Mathieu that he will "do his duty as a husband."

Mathieu soon finds himself entirely alone. For Ivich, who has evidently come to despise him as much as does Marcelle, fails in her examinations and goes back to the provinces. The volume ends with these words:

Mathieu watched Daniel disappear and thought: "I remain alone." Alone but no freer than before. He had said to himself last evening: "If only Marcelle did not exist." But in saying so he deceived himself. "No one has interfered with my freedom; my life has drained it dry." He shut the window and went back into the room. The scent of Ivich still hovered in the air. He inhaled the air, and reviewed that day of tumult. "A lot of fuss for nothing," he thought. For nothing: this life had been given him for nothing; he was nothing and yet he would not change: he was as he was made. . . . He yawned: he had finished the day, and he had also finished with his youth. Various well-bred moralities already discreetly offered him their services —disillusioned epicureanism, smiling tolerance, resignation, common sense, stoicism—all the aids whereby a man may savour, minute by minute, like a connoisseur, the failure of a life. . . . He yawned again as he repeated to himself: "It's true, it's absolutely true: I have attained the age of reason."[2]

The events of the next two volumes prove the ending of *L'Age de raison* to be an ironical one. Mathieu is still deceiving himself; still looking for liberty in remaining uncommitted, still believing he "is as he is made." He is older, that is all, not more mature. He remains as irresolute as ever. He "decides" to go to fight in Spain, but never gets there; he is "on the point of" sleeping with his sister-in-law, Odette, who is in love with him; but his call-up papers, sent out during the Munich crisis, summon him away "too soon." Walking across the Pont Neuf, he "decides" to commit suicide; but he turns back: "Next time, perhaps," he says.

Mathieu reaches his regiment, and in the third volume, *La Mort dans l'âme*, which takes place during May and June of 1940, we find him at the front. His regiment is deserted by its officers as the Germans advance; and the men, who are demoralised and think only of going home, get drunk as they wait for the Armistice. Then there appears in the village where Mathieu's unit is billeted a platoon from a first-class regiment of Chasseurs. There is no question of *these* men giving up easily or of their officers deserting them. Impressed by their soldierly qualities, Mathieu and a working-class friend persuade the Chasseurs to let them join them on a church tower, where they are making a last stand against the enemy.

Up in the tower, doomed to be destroyed by the Germans, the ineffectual Mathieu has a last hour of spectacular action:

He made his way to the parapet and stood there firing. This was revenge on a big scale. Each one of his shots avenged some ancient scruple. "One for Lola, whom I dared not rob; one for Marcelle, whom I ought to have left in the lurch; one for Odette, whom I didn't want to kiss. This for the books I never dared to write, this for the journeys I never made, this for everybody in general whom I wanted to hate and tried to understand." He fired, and the tables of the Law crashed about him. Thou Shalt Love Thy Neighbour as Thyself—bang! in that bugger's face; Thou Shalt Not Kill—bang! at that scarecrow opposite. He was firing on his fellow men, on Virtue, on the whole world. Liberty is Terror. The *mairie* was ablaze, his head was ablaze. Bullets were whining round him free in the air. "The world is going up in smoke and me with it. . . ."

Mathieu went on firing. He fired. He was cleansed. He was all-powerful; He was free.[3]

One might easily misunderstand Sartre's intentions in bringing Mathieu to such an end. The whole atmosphere of this section of the novel is exceedingly "heroic." The cowardice of those who do not want to fight is seen through stern, contemptuous eyes. The soldierly qualities of the Chasseurs are plainly held up for admiration, and in Mathieu's death there is a slightly vulgar touch of Kipling, or rather of a Hollywood war film. However, as Sartre's shrewd critic Philip Thody has pointed out, Mathieu is not meant to be a "Hero of the Last Cartridge or Cad who Made Good"; he is meant to be "the incarnation of what Hegel called 'terrorist liberty'."[4] Mathieu dies *thinking* he is free at last; but this, in the eyes of his creator, is only the last of Mathieu's many mistakes. It is *not* true for Sartre that "Liberty is Terror." So Mathieu, who brooded much about freedom, and cared for it so much, has died bravely enough, but without discovering what freedom really is.

Sartre's other central character in *Les Chemins de la liberté*, Daniel, is also left with his central problem unsolved. For Daniel is a pederast. Or rather he is not a pederast for himself; he is a pederast in the eyes of others. On the one hand, he wants to deny his homosexuality, to pretend that he is merely "different." On the other hand, since he cannot escape being seen as a homosexual, that is being objectified as a homosexual by the look of the Other, Daniel yearns to *be* a homosexual as a material object an object; to put an end to his feeling of guilt by ending his feelings altogether. "To be a stone," he dreams, "motionless, without feeling, blind. . . . To be a pederast as an oak is an oak. To be extinguished. To put out the inner eye." But, of course, Daniel's dream cannot come true. A consciousness cannot be other than conscious; a man cannot exist other than as a subjectivity, a transcendence, a being for-itself.

F

So Daniel follows the way of life of a guilt-ridden
pederast, punishing himself (if such a Freudian idiom is
permissible in summarising a Sartrian story) and punishing others. But Daniel's attempts at self-punishment are
ineffective. He makes up his mind to kill the cats he
loves, then turns back; he decides to castrate himself,
then changes his mind. He goes through with the
marriage to Marcelle (largely out of spite towards
Mathieu), but while he is on honeymoon with her, he is
at the same time physically repelled by her female body
and excited by the young male body of a gardener, and
he leaves her. Daniel's guilt and bad faith also expresses
itself in the form of unctious and priggish condemnation
of other people's conduct, including that of his fellow
homosexuals.

There is a remarkable scene in a pin-table saloon,
which brilliantly illustrates both Daniel's bad faith and
the Sartrian theory of "the look." Daniel goes into the
saloon with the idea of picking up one of the youths who
frequent it, and are to be had for money. While he is
surveying the boys appreciately, an elderly queer enters
the place and quickly makes a date with one of them.
Daniel feels "invigorated by a dry, delicious anger"
against the newcomer, and decides to punish him. He
plans to follow him when he leaves; he fancies that it
would be a good idea to impersonate a detective and take
the old man's name, and "reduce him to a state of jitters."
Just as he is relishing in anticipation the distress of his
victim, Daniel hears himself being addressed from behind.
One of his former lovers, Bobby, has been watching him
unseen. Then as Bobby comes up to him, the old gentle-
man turns and looks; seeing Daniel standing there with a
vulgar youth at his side, he smiles knowingly. Daniel is
more furious than ever. "It had to happen," Daniel
thinks. "He sees me with this tart and takes me for a
colleague." Daniel hates what he calls the "freemasonry
of the urinal": "They imagine everyone's in it. I, for one,

would sooner kill myself than look like that old sodomite."

In his bad faith, Daniel becomes converted to Christianity, but his religion turns out to be just as much a fraud as his marriage. His moment of rejoicing comes at last with the Fall of France. When he returns to Paris and sees nearly everybody running away in a panic before the German advance, Daniel experiences a thrill of real satisfaction:

For twenty years he had been on trial. There had been spies even beneath the bed. Every passer-by had been a witness for the prosecution, a judge, or both at once; every word he spoke could have been used in evidence against him. And now, in a flash—stampede.[5]

The people who had condemned him as a pederast being thus in full flight, a great weight is lifted from Daniel. The Others have been routed. Daniel smiles on the handsome sunburned German soldiers as their tanks bring them into the deserted boulevards. He wanders down to the Seine, and there, by chance encounters a good-looking young French soldier, Philippe, an unhappy pacifist, on the point of committing suicide. With his "long pederastic patience," Daniel persuades Philippe to change his mind, and deploying now, without the usual sense of guilt, the old techniques of seduction, Daniel takes Philippe back to his flat, and prepares to initiate him into homosexual practices by teaching him how to be free. Philippe asks him how he can teach him freedom.

"We must begin," Daniel said with an air of gay excitement, "by liquidating all moral values. Are you a student?"

"I was," said Philippe.

"Law?"

"No, literature."

"So much the better. In that case you will be able

to understand what I am going to say: systematic
doubt—see what I mean? Rimbaud's 'deliberate
disorganisation.' We must set about a complete process
of destruction, but not merely in words—in acts.
Everything you have borrowed from others will then
go up in smoke."[6]

This is the last we hear of Daniel and Philippe, but we
may suppose that their relationship will develop, and
finish, like that between young Lucien and the pederast
Bergère in Sartre's early short story "L'Enfance d'un
chef," where the hero's experience of abnormality only
makes him want more than ever to be normal, and so to
end up as a bourgeois Fascist. Again we may be sure that
any sort of freedom Philippe could learn about from
Daniel would be an even greater mockery than anything
that Mathieu thinks he has attained.

Besides Daniel and Mathieu, there is one other person-
ality who stands out in each volume of Les Chemins de la
liberté, and whose "way to freedom" is particularly
interesting, although his, too, is seen as a false way. This
character is Brunet, a devoted, earnest, if disastrously
naïve member of the Communist Party. Brunet is one of
those who think the question of liberty is solved in the
Marxist definition of the word as "the recognition of
necessity." Early in the story, Brunet tries to persuade
Mathieu to join the C.P. "You have renounced everything in order to be free," Brunet tells him. "Take one
step further; renounce your freedom and everything shall
be added unto you."

Politics is plain sailing for Brunet during the years of
the anti-Fascist united front, and even after the Nazi-
Soviet Pact, he continues to rely uncritically on the
wisdom of the Communist leaders. A soldier, he allows
himself to be taken prisoner by the advancing German
army, and then sets about organising a Communist cell
in the prison camp. He is distressed by the individual

self-seeking and general spinelessness of the average French soldier, and is impatient for the Germans to start persecuting them so that the anti-Nazi spirit may be revived.

In the prison-camp Brunet meets and makes friends with a mysterious intellectual named Schneider, who seems to know all about Communism and who tries to undermine Brunet's faith in the Party leadership. What is more, Schneider's predictions about political developments are verified by events. When the extent of the Russo-German *rapprochement* is revealed, and *L'Humanité* comes out again with Nazi permission, all Brunet's efforts to create an anti-Nazi movement in the camp are shown to have been wasted. Schneider is revealed as one Vicarios, a well-known Marxist writer who left the Party as a protest against the Nazi-Soviet Pact. Brunet does his best to adapt himself to the new party-line, but his emotional attachment to Schneider-Vicarios has now become so great that he decides to join with him in escaping. Other Communists in the camp, however, betray them to the Germans, and Vicarios is shot while trying to escape. He dies in Brunet's arms:

"It's the Party that's killed me," Vicarios said.

Brunet murmured: let him not die. But he knew that Vicarios was dying. . . . No power of man could efface that absolute of suffering. It was the Party which had killed him. Even if the Soviet Union won, men were alone. Brunet leaned forward; he plunged his hand in Vicarios's dirty hair, and cried as if he might yet palliate the horror, as if two lost men could, at the last moment, conquer solitude.

To hell with the Party! You are my only friend."

Vicarios did not hear. . . .[7]

Vicarios is dead. The novel breaks off with Brunet walking back to the German guards, and contemplating the lifetime of despair that lies ahead of him. We leave

Brunet, as we leave Roquentin, on the brink of salvation. But of his future we learn nothing. Throughout the story, until the last scene with Vicarios, Brunet embodies, as Sartre himself put it, the kind of man who has fled into the ready-made values of the Communist Party as an escape from the anguish of moral choice.[8]

Thus we may say of Sartre's unfinished *Les Chemins de la liberté* that *none* of the "ways to freedom" which his several characters pursue is, in his opinion, the correct way, though perhaps the reader will have learned something, by a process of contradiction and elimination about that direction in which Sartre *does* think the road to freedom lies.

REFERENCES

1. *A.R.*, p. 112 (107).
2. *A.R.*, pp. 308–9 (300).
3. *M.A.*, p. 193.
4. Quoted in Thody, p. 58.
5. *M.A.*, p. 101.
6. *M.A.*, p. 163.
7. *Les Temps modernes* (Paris), Dec. 1949, p. 1039.
8. See Thody, p. 61.

CHAPTER VIII

SARTRE'S ETHICS

Many readers must have been disappointed that Sartre did not finish *Les Chemins de la liberté*. The unwritten chapters were to have dealt with the Resistance period, concerning which he would be expected to have much of interest to relate. Questioned about his decision in an interview with Kenneth Tynan for *The Observer*, Sartre explained that he had abandoned the book precisely because its subject, the heroic Resistance years, had come to seem to him artistically unsuitable:

> The situation was too simple. I don't mean that it is simple to be courageous and risk one's life; what I mean is that the choice was too simple. One's allegiances were obvious. Since then things have become much more complicated, and more romantic in the literary sense of the term. There are many more intrigues and cross-currents. To write a novel whose hero dies in the Resistance, committed to the idea of liberty, would be much too easy.[1]

One can appreciate the point that Sartre is making here. He wrote a play about Resistance heroes, *Morts sans sépulture*, and it is easily the worst he has done. But the reasons for the abortion of Sartre's fourth volume (*La Dernière chance*, it was going to be called) may, perhaps, have been rather more complex than his answer to Tynan suggests. There is a profound contradiction in Sartre's moral theory; and by 1949, when he was supposed to be finishing *Les Chemins de la liberté*, he had reached a point where he had either to confront this contradiction, and resolve it, or abandon any work which would oblige him to make an unambiguous statement of his ethical position. It is significant that *La Dernière chance* is not the only book of Sartre's which has been advertised, but never written. The other is an exposition of "moral perspectives" which he promised, as early as 1943, in the last paragraph of *L'Etre et le néant*, and of which no more has been heard.

The contradiction I speak of is sharply evident if one compares the views put forward in *L'Etre et le néant* with those advanced in Sartre's lecture to the Club Maintenant in 1945, and afterwards published as *L'Existentialisme est un humanisme*, a short book which has enjoyed a wide sale both in the original and in English translation (as *Existentialism and Humanism*). I have already noted Sartre's conclusions in *L'Etre et le néant* (*a*) that we shall never achieve, in our relations with other people, mutual recognition of each others' freedom; (*b*) that the Kantian principle of treating other persons as ends is unattainable, and (*c*) that the essence of relations between conscious beings is not the *Mitsein* (togetherness, community, mutuality) but conflict. In *L'Existentialisme est un humanisme* Sartre advances the contrary opinion that we can, should, and indeed must, respect the freedom of others. Here he says: "I cannot make my own freedom my aim unless I make the freedom of others equally my aim."[2] In the same argument he introduces the very notion of community which he has previously rejected. Sartre is here attempting to explain his view that freedom is the foundation of all values: this, he says, simply means

that the actions of men of good faith have, as their ultimate significance, the quest of freedom itself as such. A man who belongs to some communist or revolutionary society wills certain concrete ends, which imply the will to freedom, but that freedom is willed in community. We will freedom for freedom's sake, in and through particular circumstances. And in thus willing freedom, we discover that it depends entirely upon the freedom of others, and that the freedom of others depends upon our freedom."[3]

Sartre links this point about the interdependence of freedom with *engagement* or commitment: "once there is commitment I am obliged to will the liberty of others at the same time as my own."[4] In the same lecture he tries to clarify this notion of commitment. He says that when a man chooses for himself he chooses for all men. For in the very act of choosing and preferring a man confers value on something; and in thus creating value, a man acts, so to speak, in the presence of the whole of mankind. He is therefore responsible to the whole of mankind for the evaluation he has made. For example, if I join a Catholic trade union, my action is a commitment for the whole of mankind, for in doing it I affirm the universal value of the Catholic ethos. If I marry, I bear witness to monogamy as a universal principle. In fashioning myself I fashion man. Sartre continues:

This may enable us to understand what is meant by such terms—perhaps a little grandiloquent—as anguish, abandonment and despair. . . . The existentialist frankly states that man is an anguish. His meaning is as follows: When a man commits himself to anything, fully realising that he is not only choosing what he will be, but is thereby a legislator deciding for the whole of mankind—in such a moment a man cannot escape from the sense of complete and profound responsibility. There are many, indeed, who show no such anxiety. But we affirm that they are merely disguising their anguish or are in flight from it. Certainly, many people think that in what they are doing they commit no one but themselves to anything: and if you ask them "What would happen if everyone did so?" they shrug their shoulders and reply "Everyone does not do so." But in truth, one ought always to ask of oneself what would happen if everyone did as one is doing; nor can one escape from that disturbing thought except by a kind of self-deception.[5]

Sartre compares the moral predicament of man with that of a general who has to make decisions on which the life and death of many will depend. Such leaders make their choices in anguish. And it is just this kind of anguish which existentialism describes as being common to us all as free beings and "makes explicit through direct responsibility towards other men who are concerned."[6]

The views put forward in this lecture are likely to be found more congenial by most readers than the theory of human relations put forward in *L'Etre et le néant*. The text of the lecture is also very much simpler than that of Sartre's long book. On the other hand, the ideas in *L'Existentialisme est un humanisme* are advanced with the most perfunctory of arguments, whereas the conclusions of *L'Etre et le néant* are worked out with great elaboration. Moreover, Sartre himself has expressed dissatisfaction with the lecture.

Here we have the authority of Francis Jeanson's book *Le Problème moral et la pensée de Sartre*, published in 1947 with a *lettre-préface* by Sartre himself, who commends the book wholeheartedly and informs Jeanson, among other things, that "you have so perfectly seized the development of my thinking that you have gone beyond the position taken in my books at the very moment that I have gone beyond it myself."[7] Jeanson's explanation of *L'Existentialisme est un humanisme* is that, in a lecture designed to answer the critics of the ethical aspects of existentialism, Sartre had put forward in a "strongly aggressive" way the most revolutionary aspect "of what might eventually become a Sartrist moral theory," but that this was a moral theory which was "not yet elaborated." For this reason Sartre himself considered his own lecture "as an error."[8]

This is not the only complication. For in *L'Etre et le néant* there is a singular footnote attached to the page where the author concludes that there is no escaping from the two "fundamental attitudes" towards others (i.e., the attitude tending towards masochism and the attitude tending towards sadism). The footnote reads: "These considerations do not exclude the possibility of an ethics of deliverance and salvation. But this can be achieved only after a radical conversion which we cannot discuss here."[9]

The presence of this footnote does nothing to solve the difficulty; it rather serves to underline the contradiction which lies at the heart of *L'Être et le néant* itself. For Sartre tries in that book to maintain at the same time that men are entirely free and also that men's relations with others must take one or other of two very limited and closely defined forms. And this is manifestly illogical. For if Sartre's theory of human relations is true, man cannot be entirely free. What is more, if this theory is true, there is no room for a conversion, "radical" or otherwise.

Thus there is not only a contradiction between Sartre's recommendation in *L'Existentialisme est un humanisme* that we should respect the freedom of others and his view in *L'Etre et le néant* that men cannot respect the freedom of others; there is also the contradiction in *L'Etre et le néant* between his doctrine of human freedom and his theory of human relationships.

My own view of this matter is that the theory of human relationships put forward in *L'Etre et le néant* is false. Our relations with other people do often take the forms Sartre describes—probably more often than we realise, but they also often take forms which are *not* comprehended in the categories his theory allows; and the common experience of mankind proves the possibility of those sorts of relationship which Sartre says are impossible, namely friendship, co-operation, affection, and kinds of love other than the desire to make oneself loved. And indeed Sartre himself, at the very point where *Les Chemins de la liberté* breaks off, came to depict a relationship of precisely this kind which *L'Etre et le néant* excludes.

The relationships in the first three volumes of the tetralogy—those between Mathieu and Marcelle and Ivich and Daniel, between Daniel and Marcelle and Philippe, between Boris and Lola: all these and the rest can be seen as variants of psychological conflict or struggle. But the relationship between Brunet and Vicarios described in the unfinished fourth volume is of another order. Their "Strange Friendship," as the title calls it, is a real friendship. The obvious homosexual element is transfigured into a sort of idealised Platonic attachment. When Brunet plunges his hand into the dirty hair of the dying Vicarios and cries out in his "absolute of suffering" that his friend—his only friend—may not die, we meet also an absolute of togetherness. Assuredly, in the best tradition of romantic literature, their relationship is ended by death: but it achieves its moment of truth, and that moment is a refutation of the theory of human relations in *L'Etre et le néant*.

So we may attach a further significance to Sartre's abandonment of *Les Chemins de la liberté*. Not only has he turned away from this novel when the time has come for him to make a positive statement of his concept of liberty, even as he sent Orestes away from Argos as soon as he had killed the King and the Queen. Sartre has also reached the point of an implicit repudiation of the psychology of *L'Etre et le néant*, but stops short of an explicit repudiation. Since 1949 Sartre has retreated from these problems of personal ethics and relationships into the altogether more general sphere of politics and sociology.

Admittedly, while ceasing to write novels, he has continued to write plays. But the dramatist does not do the same work as the novelist. The novelist is concerned with analysis and with the inwardness of human experience; he speaks as one man to one reader. The method of the play is dialectical rather than analytical. The dramatist addresses a sort of public meeting, his audience; and he addresses it through exteriority—that is, through simulated action and spoken words. The audience must put its own interiority on what it sees and hears. What is more, the theatre as a social institution is a far more effective medium than fiction for the expression of political ideas. All the plays Sartre has written since *Huis clos* have been political plays. Politics, or more precisely, socialism has become Sartre's chief, indeed his all-pervasive concern. The phrase "committed literature" (*la littérature engagée*), which he made famous, meant, as he originally defined it, literature committed to any genuinely moral view of life, no matter what. Indeed it could not be defined otherwise on the existentialist postulate that every man must be the maker of his own moral values. But "committed literature" was soon being used by Sartre himself and other Left-wing critics who took up the phrase to mean "literature committed to socialism" as if no other commitment could possibly be genuine.

I myself admire Sartre for his socialist commitment, for his unfailing readiness as a celebrated writer, to give an intellectual lead on public problems. One cannot but respect his concern for the common good, and his *seriousness*—so unlike the ruinous *légèreté* of Shaw and equally unlike that *esprit de sérieux*, or pompous earnestness, which Sartre himself detests in the bourgeoisie. And yet in the very intensity of his socialism one can discern an element of what Sartre himself would call *évasion*, a flight from the contradictions of his analysis of personal relations into a philosophy which does not reckon in individuals, but in masses.

It is no accident that Sartre's own favourite critic should be Francis Jeanson, a Marxist. Jeanson does not like the "ontology" of *L'Etre et le néant* because it is too obviously at variance with Marxism; nor does he like the ethics of *L'Existentialisme est un humanisme*, because it is too close to Kant. Therefore he picks on the footnote about "radical conversion," and interprets the theory of human relationships set forth in *L'Etre et le néant* as an account of what relations are at what he calls the "level" of individualism, the "level" of "the primitive concern for coincidence with self";[10] and then goes on to suggest that Sartre's notion of conversion points to what human relations *could be* if life were lived at a different level: and this different level for Jeanson is that of Marxist collectivism. So we find that Jeanson, in his first book on Sartre, sees Marxism as a solution to Sartre's dilemma; and in his second book on Sartre (*Sartre par lui-même*, published in 1956) he congratulates him on the progress he has made in that direction.

Jeanson's talk about "levels" is hardly satisfactory as serious philosophy; but he writes as a man who knows Sartre well, and his insight into the development of Sartre's thinking has proved to be much more exact than that of those Marxist critics, such as Lukács, who have attacked Sartre's existentialism as being itself a kind of bourgeois nihilism. Sartre has become more and more of a Marxist as time has gone by. His earlier statements of socialism were rather of the social-democratic, even of a somewhat utopian kind. Thus, for example, we find in *Qu'est-ce que la littérature?* (published in 1947) a plea for a classless society as a means of reconciling the writer to his public. In that essay, after speaking of the alienation of the writer from the reader in bourgeois societies, Sartre argues that only in a classless society could literature realise its full essence. For if all men were readers, if the reading public was made up of society as a whole, the writer could write about the life of man in general, and there would be no difference between his subject and his public. In the same essay Sartre says that for the writer to be free, he must not only be free to say what he wishes, he must write for a public which is free to change its structure:

Thus in a society without classes, without dictatorship and without stability, literature would end by becoming conscious of itself; it would understand that form and content, public and subject, are identical; that the formal freedom of saying and the material freedom of doing complete each other; that it best manifests the subjectivity of the person when it translates most deeply collective needs and reciprocally that its function is to express the concrete universal to the concrete universal, and that its end is to appeal to the freedom of men so that they may realise and maintain the reign of human freedom.[11]

Sartre admits that this vision is "utopian," but he adds: "It has allowed us to perceive the conditions under which literature might manifest itself in its fullness and purity."[12] The argument here is very close to that of *L'Existentialisme est un humanisme*; Sartre's belief in socialism is part of his belief in liberty. In 1945, when Sartre brought out the first number of his literary and political monthly, *Les Temps modernes*, it did not much matter in France what kind of socialist a man was. For those were the days of Left-wing unity. Sartre's early collaborators included such diverse socialists as Raymond Aron, Maurice Merleau-Ponty and Albert Camus. But this co-operation did not last long. The Communist Party constituted too much of a problem. The Party was hostile to Sartre; and his hostility to the Party was manifest enough in the story of Brunet and Vicarios, the victims of the Party, in *Les Chemins de la liberté*. In 1949, Sartre started a political party of his own, the Democratic Revolutionary Rally, to forward the cause of independent socialism in France. The movement attracted some support among intellectuals but none whatever from the working class. From its failure Sartre drew a harsh lesson. As the Communist Party had been proved to be the only effective party in France dedicated to the realisation of

socialism, he felt he was obliged, however much he dis-
liked its methods, to support it. Henceforth Sartre became
a close fellow-traveller with the Communist Party; and
though he stopped short of joining its ranks, he defended
it as the one strong agency in France for the cause of
socialism and of peace. Though he lost most of his
independent socialist friends in the process, Sartre would
brook no more attacks on the Party or on Russia. Only
once did he rebel against the line: in 1956 he made a
vigorous protest against the Soviet action in Hungary on
the grounds that intervention was neither necessary for
nor even conducive to the safety of socialism. For the rest,
both before and after Budapest, Sartre has been an
energetic champion of the achievements of Russia, China,
Cuba and other Communist countries, and a bitter critic
of America and the West.

In 1960 Sartre brought out an even longer theoretical
book than *L'Etre et le néant*. This was Volume I of his
Critique de la raison dialectique. In this work, which he calls
"anthropological," Sartre's subject is man in the mass, as
opposed to man the individual; and collective relations
instead of personal relations. Although it is impossible to
form a complete impression until Volume II has appeared,
a few important points may be touched upon here. The
author is attempting to work out a new kind of Marxism,
that is to say a Marxism revitalised by existentialism.
There is no doubt here that Sartre is now giving Marxism
priority over existentialism. Marxism, he says, is a
"philosophy," whereas existentialism is only an "ideology." He explains what he means by this distinction.
"Philosophies" are those great creative systems which
cannot be transcended until history has moved on in
some respect. In the modern world, the great creative
philosophical moments are represented by Descartes and
Locke; then by Kant and Hegel; and in our own time by
Marx. Thus Marxism is still *the* philosophical system of
the present because we have not moved beyond it. What

Sartre calls the "idéologue" is a much humbler person than the philosopher; the former merely develops the great original systems of the latter, he "exploits the domain." Thus in calling existentialism an ideology, Sartre defines it as a "parasitic system that lives on the margin of the knowledge to which it was at first opposed, but to which it now attempts to integrate itself."[13] In other words, Sartre now sees existentialism as "wishing to integrate itself" into Marxism.

This is not to say that existentialism is ready to be swallowed up at once by Marxism. But "from the day the Marxist quest assumes the human dimension, existentialism will no longer have a *raison d'être*." Meanwhile Sartre believes that the integration of existentialism with Marxism can bring about the modernisation which Marxism badly needs. He claims that Marxism has lost its theoretical basis; its concepts are "diktats"; its spokesmen are far too abstract, rigid, and out of touch with actual experience; they are bogged down in out-of-date psychology and metaphysics, without being aware of their own teleology. A matter on which Sartre lays stress is, as one might expect, determinism. He wants Marxism to purge itself of its nineteenth-century materialistic concept of determinism and accept from existentialism a rational concept of human freedom. In doing so, Sartre does not think Marxists would be violating the spirit of Marx's own teaching. Sartre takes as his text a remark of Engels: "Men make their history themselves, but in a given environment which conditions them."[14] Sartre stresses the words that "men make their history"; it is *they* who make it, not History—not the Past—which makes them. Thus Sartre would have us believe that he is out to achieve a purification of Marxism rather than a dilution of it by the assimilation of existentialist insights.

The rest of this volume is largely taken up with a study of mass relations. Here we immediately notice a contrast not only between what Sartre says and what is usually

G

said by Marxist writers, but also between what Sartre
says here and what he says about individual personal
relations in *L'Etre et le néant*. Conflict is no longer said to
be a fundamental condition of human relations. It is still
seen as a basic factor in human history. For according to
Sartre's anthropology, societies pass from being "col-
lectives" to being "groups," from being individualistic,
atomistic "pluralities of solitudes" to being organic
united wholes. The process of fusion is dialectical, and
the group is held together not only by the oath or pledge
(of the social contract) but by Terror. It is violence, he
says, which unites the group until it has become inte-
grated and acquired institutions. "The communal
freedom creates itself as Terror."[15] Nevertheless conflict
is now seen as a secondary and curable condition. Sartre
gives a new reason for it, namely *scarcity*. It is the shortage
of food and other materials in the world which brings
about the struggle between man and man. This makes
human violence understandable and, so to speak,
rational. Sartre is now opposing the view that conflict
between men arises from aggressive forces in human
nature itself, as Hobbes and Freud and others think.
Sartre claims that there is no need for war between men;
and that there have been such wars only because there
has been such scarcity.

"The entire himan adventure, at least until now, is a
desperate struggle against scarcity,"[16] he writes. Scarcity
makes men suspicious, since each is afraid the other will
betray the social contract. Relations between them are
uneasy, even when they are not at war. Besides, the
structures which men impose on the world in order to
escape scarcity often turn back upon their inventors and
make their predicament worse.

This last situation is described by Sartre, with his usual
flair for dramatic utterance, as "the Hell of the practico-
inert." He illustrates this notion with the story of Chinese
peasants each cutting wood for his several uses and so

bringing about the deforestation of vast tracts of land, as a result of which they are all exposed to the devastating harm of flooding. Man is thus destroyed, or, if not destroyed, at least held prisoner by his own creations. Now this theory is clearly very different from that of orthodox Marxism, where men are seen as the creatures of circumstance, or of History. For Sartre the material or economic factors are still crucial, as they are for all Marxists, but he sees history as itself the creation of men. That is to say, history is the result of conscious but often shortsighted decisions made by men in face of the problem of scarcity and in face of the problems which arise from their ancestors' attempts to solve the problem of scarcity.

This first volume of the *Critique de la raison dialectique* is intended only to set forth the intelligible foundations of a "structural anthropology" as Sartre calls it; the next volume, he promises, will show us that there is one human history with one intelligible truth. The book is already exceedingly long, devious, and intricate; it is full of disconcerting jargon; it lacks the elegance of Sartre's earlier work; but while it is not always perspicuously reasoned, it is splendidly rationalistic.

REFERENCES

1. *Observer* (London), 18 Jun. 1961, p. 21.
2. *E.H.*, p. 83.
3. *E.H.*, pp. 82–3 (51–2).
4. *E.H.*, p. 83.
5. *E.H.*, pp. 27–8 (30–1.)
6. *E.H.*, p. 32 (32.)
7. Jeanson, *Le Problème moral et la pensée de Sartre*, Paris 1947, p. 13.
8. *Ibid.*
9. *E.N.*, p. 484 n. (412 n).
10. Jeanson, *op. cit.*, p. 267.
11. *Q.L.*, p. 197 (119).
12. *Ibid.*
13. *C.R.D.*, p. 18.
14. *C.R.D.*, p. 60.
15. *C.R.D.*, p. 449.
16. *C.R.D.*, p. 201.

CHAPTER IX

SARTRE ON BAUDELAIRE
AND GENET

The possibility of salvation through socialism is adumbrated by Sartre in an essay on Baudelaire, published in 1946. This is one of those books common enough in the present century, in which literary criticism is boldly, if not always wisely, combined with psycho-analysis. But the psycho-analysis (if we may so call it) of Sartre differs sharply from that of Freud because of Sartre's repudiation of the unconscious in favour of the view that all neuroses spring from a conscious choice. Besides, Freud's psycho-analysis is primarily a technique for curing disorders. Sartre's psycho-analysis is an explanatory theory, and it offers not so much an alternative therapy to that of Freud, as an alternative reading of a neurotic case history. Sartre's reading of Baudelaire's biography is all the more interesting because of certain resemblances we may notice (but must not over-emphasise) between the childhood of the poet and that of Sartre himself. Sartre attributes great significance to the fact that Baudelaire's father died when the poet was six years old. (Sartre's own father died when he was two.) Between Baudelaire and his widowed mother there grew up, Sartre observes, a bond of mutual adoration. Mme Baudelaire was at once her son's idol and his comrade. He was indeed so enveloped by her that he scarcely existed as a separate person. And precisely because he was so absorbed in a being who appeared to exist "by necessity and divine right," the young Baudelaire was protected from all uneasiness. His mother was his Absolute.

But Baudelaire's mother remarried and the boy was sent to a boarding school. This, says Sartre, was the turning-point in the poet's life. (We should observe that Baudelaire was only seven when *his* mother remarried; Sartre was twelve when his mother took that step.) It was then that Baudelaire was "thrown into a personal existence." His Absolute had been taken from him. The justification for his existence had gone. He was alone, and in his solitude he discovered that life had been given him "for nothing." It was at this point also, according to Sartre, that Baudelaire made his mistake. The poet concluded that he was *destined* to be "for ever alone." In fact, says Sartre, we may here discern the *original choice* of Baudelaire. Baudelaire *decided* to be (as he put it) "éternellement solitaire." He did not *discover* any destiny; because, of course, for Sartre there is no destiny to discover. Baudelaire, in his freedom, *chose* solitude; he *claimed* solitude. He wanted it, because he wanted to feel unique.

This is something which Sartre distinguishes from ordinary children's discovery of subjectivity. They too discover the meaning of the ego or *le Moi*. But they do not brood upon it. Baudelaire, "who discovers himself in despair, anger, and jealousy, will base his whole life on the stagnant meditation of his formal singularity."[1] Baudelaire's choice, says Sartre, is a form of pride. He is like Narcissus. Where the ordinary man looks at a tree and sees a tree, Baudelaire can only see himself looking at a tree. He is aware only of his consciousness of himself. But what he sees is not an object, since the self is not an object. For this reason his biography is bound to be the story of a defeat. It is the defeat of Narcissus, who gazes at his own image, but can never touch, or get at himself. Hence his boredom, disgust, nausea, vertigo.

Sartre notes how Baudelaire escapes from this feeling of vertigo into literary creation. But the trouble is, says Sartre, that the poet does not extend his creativeness to the realm of moral principles. Baudelaire simply accepts the bourgeois Catholic ethics of his mother and his step-father. The result, since he does not lead the life that the bourgeoisie approves of, is that Baudelaire is possessed by an acute feeling of guilt. Sartre's argument is that if Baudelaire had rejected the parental moral code, and worked out a new morality of his own, he could have been saved.

As it was, Baudelaire yearned always for the family and absolute security that his mother had given him in in-fancy. In truth, Sartre insists, life demands maturity; we must accept the fact that we cannot have for ever the security of the happy child. Baudelaire's disease was not (as a Freudian might say) the Oedipus complex; it was a "theological complex by which he assimilated his parents to divinities."[2] Baudelaire's problem is that he cannot grow up. He makes a cult of sin. He remains uncommitted to anything or anybody. He will not take responsibility for the world he lives in. He wants to be an object that exists; but all his self-analysis stops short of self-know-ledge. Thus Baudelaire came to hate both himself and humanity. In poetic creation he could avoid any sort of *giving*, which he detested. "In writing a poem, he felt he was giving nothing to men, or, at any rate, nothing more than a useless object."[3]

Sartre has further reproaches to address to Baudelaire. The poet's fault was not only that he resisted any kind of commitment, but that he resisted any kind of *socialist* commitment. First Baudelaire acquiesced in the morals of the bourgeoisie, and then he also acquiesced in the reactionary politics of the Second Empire. All the poet cared about, says Sartre, was to be "different." Sartre contrasts this attitude with that of George Sand, Hugo, Marx, Proudhon, and Michelet—the progressive writers of the nineteenth century who taught men that the future could be controlled, and society changed for the better. Baudelaire, with his Narcissism, his dandyism, his foolish "diabolism," played the game of the extreme Catholic reactionaries.

Baudelaire is one of the best-written of Sartre's essays, but it is undoubtedly also one of the cases where his puritanism becomes, as puritanism is apt to become, philistine. In what is supposed to be a piece of literary criticism, the thought that Baudelaire was a great poet is given no consideration. Sartre fastens instead on Baudelaire's remark about a poem being an "objet inutile," as if this were the supreme truth. One has the impression, as Mr Thody says, that Sartre "would have preferred Baudelaire to have been a third-rate early Socialist pamphleteer rather than a first-rate lyrical poet."[4] But one must not be unfair to Sartre. Even in his most enthusiastic Left-wing moments he has resisted the aesthetic prejudices of ordinary Marxists. At the East-West Round Table of the Société Européenne de Culture at Venice in 1956, he vigorously defended such writers as Proust, Joyce, and Kafka against Communist charges of "decadence" and "subjectivism."[5] Moreover Sartre returned to the notion of salvation through art in a book he wrote some six years after *Baudelaire*; this time, in fact he analysed the case of a man who was so saved (Roquentin was left at the end of *La Nausée* with the prospect of such salvation, but not in the actual enjoyment of it). I refer here to Sartre's essay on Jean Genet, published in 1952 as *Saint Genet, comédien et martyr*; since Genet was already known to the French public as a thief, traitor, pederast and pornographic author, this title may be seen as yet another example of Sartre's flair for a sensational phrase.

Once more literary criticism is combined with existentialist psycho-analysis, and indeed (for the book is much longer than *Baudelaire*) with a great deal of discursive, ill-organised but intensely readable social and moral criticism. The case history is undoubtedly remarkable. Genet is a bastard, a foundling; from an orphanage he was sent to be brought up by foster-parents, who

were peasants in Morvan. Only naturally, being deprived
of maternal love, of status, of rights—especially, in
Sartre's view, of rights which are so exalted in peasant
society (Sartre has always regarded the Lockian concept
of rights as one of the greatest evils of bourgeois moral
thinking)—Genet stole things. One day he was found
out. People said: "Genet is the *Thief*." When he heard
that "vertiginous word," as Sartre calls it, Genet decided
that he must be what he was said to be. Henceforth he
was the Thief. In the terminology of *L'Etre et le néant*,
Genet decided to live out the existence of that being into
which the look of the Other had objectified him. He lived
a life of crime; he went in and out of reformatories and
prisons. Then he transcended his experiences by making
them the material of literature.

This is the story of a salvation, not of a conversion.
The criminal becomes a poet, but remains a criminal; he
is a criminal-poet. As Sartre says, what is important
about Genet is that he wrote, not *about* a thief and a
pederast, but *as* a thief and pederast. He is entirely open,
and unashamed; his books are completely authentic. This
time Sartre does not overlook the fact, as he does in the
case of Baudelaire, that the poet is marvellously talented.
But what interests him about Genet, is that in writing so
frankly as a criminal, and writing so well, Genet has a
highly disturbing effect on the "right-thinking bourgeois"
public. Genet makes the reader feel his homosexual
desires, he communicates the thrill of his criminal life. He
compels one, in this sense, to be his accomplice. Oscar
Wilde said of pornography that it holds up to the reader
his own shame. Sartre says the same of Genet's writings.
They reveal to the "right-thinking bourgeois" truths
from which the bourgeois is trying to hide.

Sartre does not fail to relish the irony of Genet's career.
The bourgeois persecute the little bastard, make him
their scapegoat; but the scapegoat turns to torment them,
first as a thief (which they have named him), and then

even more effectively as a poet. Then, thanks to the publication of his books, which themselves exalt crime and vice, Genet becomes a literary celebrity. Out of respect for literature, and at the behest of a number of Left-wing intellectuals, the President of the Republic remits Genet's prison sentence. Genet's literary earnings are soon so ample that he has no incentive to steal; he becomes a prosperous bourgeois himself, noted by all who know him for his sweetness of nature and generosity; and if still a practising homosexual, he completes the new image by a discreet marriage to a motherly widow.

We may think Sartre somewhat hard on the French bourgeoisie in the grim pleasure he takes in this story. He does not observe that, in any other country but France, Genet's scandalous books would never have been published; in both the United States and England translations of his more sensational works have been suppressed; the British authorities have indeed also banned the originals despite their being printed in the decent obscurity of a foreign language. Again, it is unlikely that the Head of State in any other country but France would have consented to release a prisoner, simply because he was a poet. But there is a more serious point to be made against Sartre in this connexion. If one feels that the people who condemned little Genet, already ill-used as he was, as a criminal, and punished him so harshly, were doing an injustice, it is because one has rejected, under the influence of such men as Freud, the old-fashioned notion that children had complete free-will and were wholly responsible for their deeds. Freud, and others like him, have made us more compassionate, more understanding, less ready to blame and punish the young, precisely because they have shown us, in terms of their own "deterministic" psychology, that children with Genet's sort of history often *cannot help* doing the kind of thing that Genet did. But Sartre's psycho-analysis is directly opposed to Freud on this question. His absolute

libertarianism makes children morally responsible agents
no less surely and severely than does the free-will dogma
of Victorian Christianity. We have already seen what
Sartre says of Baudelaire: that Baudelaire at the *age of
seven* made in bad faith that original choice from which
all his later evils sprang. Sartre has very different ideas
about what is right and wrong from the peasants of
Morvan; but a man who judges one boy, as he judges
Baudelaire, is not the ideal critic of those who judge another. Sartre has spoken of the moral teaching of existentialism as "austere";* where it restores the notion of
juvenile culpability is, it can only be described as harshly
reactionary.

Sartre is open to a further criticism. He expresses the
utmost admiration for the "pure courage," "mad confidence," and "absurd resolution" with which little Genet
"wanted to be what he was without a moment's weakness"
(the italics are Sartre's). Manifestly, Genet is here being
praised for the very reason for which Baudelaire was
condemned. For Baudelaire at the same age decided *to be*
what he believed himself destined to be, "for ever alone,"
just as Genet decided *to be* what he had heard himself
called, "the thief." They want to be different kinds of
beings, assuredly, but both equally want "to be"; both
equally betray what Jeanson calls the "primitive concern
for co-incidence with self." How then, in existentialist
terms, can the one be considered admirable and the other
culpable? We may recall, in this connexion, a similar
case from Sartre's fiction: that of Lucien Fleurier in his
story "L'Enfance d'un chef." Fleurier as an adolescent
has the same yearning for existence that Sartre detects in
Baudelaire and Genet. And when, as a result of making,
largely for effect, bitter remarks about Jews, Fleurier finds

* So has Simone de Beauvoir. "People like to believe that virtue is
easy," she writes in *L'Existentialisme et la sagesse des nations*, "and they
resign themselves without much difficulty to the thought that virtue is
impossible. What they hate to realise is that it is possible but difficult."

himself described, and indeed respected by his bourgeois acquaintances as an anti-Semite, he decides *to be* what Other People have called him: he becomes a Fascist. In this case, it is abundantly clear that the author has *no* admiration for the character he is analysing. Fleurier is "out," like Baudelaire. Why then is Genet "in"?

One is bound to conclude that what Sartre admires about Genet is not his pure courage, or mad confidence, or absurd resolution *to be*; he admires him for being what he calls "the Bukharin of the bourgeoisie," the man who undermines the society which spewed him out. Other names in Sartre's gallery of heroes may be seen to be ranged with Genet. There is Gide, who affronted "the right-thinking people" by proclaiming himself publicly a pederast, and defending his sexual habits. And, of course, there is Roquentin: although he was never shown as achieving much, there was no doubt about his hatred of the bourgeois.

Thus we see the sheep divided from the goats: on the one hand, Genet, Gide, Roquentin, artists all, if not all of equal merit, and all unequivocally anti-bourgeois; on the other hand, Baudelaire and Fleurier, one an artist, the other not, but both on the side of the bourgeoisie and Fascism. The final criterion is thus, strictly speaking, neither literary nor psychological: it is political. But it cannot be said to be positively socialist. Genet was not a socialist; Gide was never consistently one; Roquentin is nowhere said to be one. It is enough or appears to be enough for Sartre that one is against the bourgeoisie. A positive vision of socialism is not demanded of those whom Sartre admires, although the lack of it is censured in those of whom he disapproves.

REFERENCES

1. *Baudelaire*, p. 23.
2. Dempsey, p. 60.
3. *Baudelaire*, pp. 220–1.
4. Thody, p. 148.
5. *Comprendre* (Venice), Sept. 1956, pp. 273–4.

CHAPTER X

POLITICAL DRAMAS

In 1948, when his attitude to the Communist Party was still openly critical, Sartre wrote one of the sharpest and most telling of modern political plays, *Les Mains sales*. In this play Hugo, a young middle-class Communist, is sent by the party to kill one of its leaders, Hoederer, who is making a pact with the Royalist and Liberal politicians of his (unnamed Balkan) country to resist the Germans. Hoederer is alleged to be selling out the workers to the old ruling class. Hugo, the appointed executioner, is a gentle idealist by nature, and ill-prepared by his upbringing to kill at point blank a man he knows. And though he tells himself that his scruples are but bourgeois inhibitions, Hugo cannot bring himself to do the job when the opportunity presents itself. A little later, however, Hugo sees Hoederer kissing his wife; then, in an access of jealousy, he finds it easy to shoot him. Afterwards, Hugo discovers that communications with Russia have been restored, and that Hoederer's policy of collaboration with the Royalists and Liberals has become the Party Line. By then it is too late to undo what has been done, and a virtue has to be made of a necessity.

The irony of this story is so deadly that many people have seen it as a purely anti-Communist play. But the author's intentions were not quite so simple. He forbade the production of the play in Vienna in 1952, when he thought it might be used as anti-Communist propaganda, and even went to Vienna in person to take part in a Communist-sponsored "Peace Congress." This, admitedly, was after the collapse of Sartre's own party, and at the time of his reconciliation with the C.P. But even though *Les Mains sales* was written at an earlier stage, the author has found nothing in it that he has ever wished to repudiate. Nor should we expect him to have done so.

The most interesting character in the piece, and the one by which the author's sympathies are most clearly engaged, is Hoederer. There is a striking contrast between Hoederer and Brunet, that slavish, naïve, unreflective follower of the Party Line. Whereas Brunet thinks that whatever Moscow says is right, Hoederer believes that a man can never be sure what is right, but must act and accept responsibility for his actions. He tells Hugo that a man who does not want to take the risk of being wrong ought not to go in for politics. When Hugo in the purity of his Communist idealism expresses horror at Hoederer's plan for a coalition with the bourgeois parties, Hoederer says:

How frightened you are of soiling your hands. All right, stay pure! Who does it help, and why did you come to us? Purity is an ideal for a fakir or a monk. You intellectuals, you bourgeois anarchists, you use it as an excuse for doing nothing. Do nothing, stay put, keep your elbows to your sides, wear kid gloves. My hands are filthy. I've dipped them up to the elbows in blood and shit. So what? Do you think you can govern and keep your spirit white?[1]

Here we are given an important insight into Sartre's own attitude to politics. Political action is necessarily a struggle—the result, as explained in the *Critique*, of scarcity. Therefore violence is inevitable. Hoederer does not want to be assassinated, but he does not object to assassination as such. Similarly we may notice in Sartre's condemnation of the Soviet intervention in Hungary in 1956 that he did not object to intervention as such; he only objected to it in circumstances where it was unnecessary for the defence of socialism. By the same token, where the consequences of an "impure policy" can be reasonably thought to be conducive to socialism, Sartre is entirely in favour of such methods.

Naturally Sartre has had an easier time attacking the enemies of socialism than he has had in defending his Communist friends. He has been an energetic critic of the American "way of life" and an equally vigorous opponent of French imperialism. His disapproval of America prompted him to write one of his best-known, but least impressive plays, *La Putain respectueuse*, which is about a prostitute who is induced to pretend that a Negro has raped her, to perjure herself in order to uphold the corrupt racialist morality of a Southern state. The unreality, and crudely propagandist conception of this play came out all the more strongly when it was made into a film.* A more effective piece of political writing for the theatre was *Nekrassov*, a satirical farce at the expense of those Western zealots for the Cold War who make use of Russian *émigrés* of the "I Chose Freedom" type to excite the public against Communism. Enjoyable as it is, *Nekrassov*, by its nature, is not a work of high artistic seriousness, like *Les Mouches* and *Huis clos*. A later, and much more elaborate attack on "Western values," *Les Séquestrés d'Altona* (first performed in 1959) was vitiated by its sheer obscurity. Profoundly disturbed by the use of torture by the French colonialists in Algeria (a concern

---

* Kenneth Tynan, interviewing Sartre for *The Observer* (25 Jun. 1961) mentioned that he had seen a simplified version of *La Putain respectueuse* in Moscow, and asked the playwright if he had authorised the changes. Sartre replied: "I didn't see the production, but I agreed to an optimistic ending, as in the film version, which was made in France. I knew too many young working-class people who had seen the play and had been disheartened because it ended sadly. And I realised that those who are really pushed to the limit, who hang on to life because they must, have need of hope." These words oblige us to read Sartre's remark about "life beginning on the other side of despair" as being addressed to the wealthier classes only.

revealed also by his preface to Henri Alleg's *La Question*),*
Sartre attempted in *Les Séquestrés d'Altona* to treat the
subject of torture indirectly, by making its central
character a former Nazi officer, Franz (a significant
name?), a man going mad in an effort to justify to himself
and to the future his own resort to torture. But the
symbolism is too heavy, and the whole thing is tricked out
with too many obvious theatrical devices, for the play to
succeed as more than highbrow melodrama, flattering
the kind of audience which likes to listen to things it
cannot understand.

One of Sartre's most interesting essays in political
drama is the scenario for a film which was never made,
and which, though published in book form in French and
English, remains an undeservedly neglected work. It is
called *L'Engrenage*, and although it was written two
years before *Les Mains sales*, it treats the same themes in
greater detail and with more humanity. The scenario
depicts the career of a revolutionary leader, Jean, who
comes to power at the head of the workers' party in a
small republic in, presumably, Central America. Jean's
country is on the frontier of a great capitalist nation, so
that even as President, he cannot do what he wishes. He
would like to nationalise the oil wells, as his party has
promised, and as his people expect him to do; but he
knows that if he does so at once the Great Power will
intervene and crush his government. His only hope is to
wait until the energies of the neighbouring state are
directed towards a war elsewhere. In the interim, which
he expects to last six years, Jean refuses to summon
parliament (which would certainly decree premature

* This book was suppressed in France in 1958. At about the same
time, Sartre's friend and critic Jeanson, a supporter of the Algerian
nationalists, fled the country; he was tried in his absence and condemned as a traitor. Sartre himself offended the French authorities by
helping to draft the "Declaration of 121 intellectuals" on behalf of
"conscientious deserters" in Algeria, but the sanctions taken against
him were trifling.

nationalisation), and he limits the freedom of the press (so that his whole policy of *attentisme* shall not be attacked and ruined).

Jean is in a tragic dilemma, because he believes passionately in a parliamentary legislation and a free press as well as in socialism; and so, doing things which he hates doing, and which no one understands, Jean's character deteriorates. Then a group of socialist militants, including some of his best friends, overthrows Jean's government; but at the end of the scenario, his successor as President is seen receiving the ambassador of the Great Power and realising that he is trapped in a position where he cannot touch the oil wells: he is compelled to govern the republic precisely as Jean had governed it.

The analogy between this scenario and the events which took place, soon afterwards in Guatemala, and fifteen years later in Cuba, is striking. We cannot say that Jean exactly foreshadows Dr Castro; but we may fancy, with Sartre, that if there had not been a Communist power behind Castro, the Americans would have frustrated his socialism by force, even as they intervened against the nascent socialism of Guatemala. And because Castro has been able to do what Jean could not do, Sartre is, not surprisingly, an eager supporter of his regime.

There are other points in *L'Engrenage* which are worth attention. There is a conflict of conscience between Jean and his bourgeois pacifist friend Lucien which resembles the difference between Hoederer and Hugo, although in this case, Jean's attitude is less harsh, and Lucien's less silly. It is Lucien who protests when Jean proposes to alter the party programme from a peaceful struggle to armed revolt; he believes one ought to be able to achieve socialism without dirtying one's hands:

"The first condition for being a man is to refuse all

participation, direct or indirect, in an act of violence,"
says Lucien.

Jean listens to him, torn between friendly admiration for Lucien's integrity, and the bitterness of his
own experience.

"And what methods would you use?" he asks

"Everything possible. Books, newspapers, theatre..."

"But you're a bourgeois all the same, Lucien. Your
father never beat your mother. He's never been
flogged by the coppers or sacked from a factory without
explanation or without notice simply because they
wanted to reduce their staff. You've never suffered
any violence. You can't feel it as we do."

"If you've suffered it," replies Lucien, "you've all
the more reason for hating it."

"Yes, but it's deep-rooted in me."[2]

There is an episode in this script which prefigures the
ironical plot of *Les Mains sales*. Jean decides that political
necessity requires him to liquidate Benga, against whom
there is circumstantial evidence of treachery, but no
proof. Over-riding the plea of Lucien, the committee
decides to have Benga shot; lots are drawn, and the task
falls to Lucien. Jean, however, relieves him of that dis-
tasteful duty, and shoots Benga himself. With his dying
breath Benga proclaims his innocence, and indeed soon
afterwards his innocence is proved.

One may be sure that *L'Engrenage* would have made a
stimulating and successful film. The regret that it was
never done is to some extent mitigated by the fact that
the author returned to the topics he deals with here, and
built them, together with others, into the most substantial and important of his post-war plays, *Le Diable et le bon
Dieu*. This is one of Sartre's best works, rich in ideas,
dialectic, drama, feeling, and never for one moment
fussy and obscure, like *Les Séquestrés d'Altona*. In *Saint
Genet* Sartre speaks in defence of the "old-fashioned

H

categories of Good and Evil", and the main theme of *Le Diable et le bon Dieu*, which came out in the same year as *Saint Genet* (1952) is precisely that: the conflict of Good and Evil. The piece is set in Germany at the time of the Peasants' Revolt and the Lutheran Reformation; its hero is Goetz, a nobleman's bastard, who proves himself at the same time the most cruel and the most successful military leader in the country. Sartre believes that as an orphan he has a special affinity with the bastard; he defines an orphan as a "false bastard"; and Genet, Kean, the illegitmate English actor (the subject of a Dumas play which Sartre refurbished for the modern stage), and now Goetz are outsize heroes for him precisely because they are *real* bastards.

In the first act of *Le Diable et le bon Dieu* we meet Goetz doing evil for its own sake. Evil appeals to him. It is his "reason for living." By the end of this act he has the town of Worms at his mercy, and, with the death of his legitimate half-brother, he finds himself the lawful owner of his father's estates. But in this moment of triumph, Goetz feels no relish of satisfaction. Heinrich, a shrewd, if also hypocritical and shifty priest (whose bad character has some charm for Goetz) persuades him that there is nothing wonderful in doing evil. The world is so impregnated with evil, that a man could deserve Hell by staying in bed. There is no need to work for damnation as Goetz does. Everyone does evil. Goetz asks him: "Does no one do only good, then?" Heinrich says: "No one." Thereupon, Goetz lays a bet that *he* will henceforth do nothing but good.

In the second act we witness the unfolding of Goetz's sacred project. He decides to begin by giving away his lands to the poor. But he is immediately asked by Nasty, the leader of the peasants' movement, to stay his hand; if he gives away his lands at once, says Nasty, he will precipitate a revolt before the time is ripe for a revolt to succeed. If Goetz acts at once, the peasants will rise without adequate preparation, and the barons will destroy them. Goetz refuses to wait; he says he cannot do Good by instalments. Besides, he is not only going to give his land away, he is going to create a model community, based entirely on fraternity and common ownership. "Thanks to me, before the year is out, happiness, love and virtue will reign over ten thousand acres of this land. On my own domains I wish to build the City of the Sun."[3]

Events which follow prove that Nasty was right, and Goetz wrong. After Goetz has built his "model village," as Nasty calls it, he has to struggle all the time against the efforts of the clergy to undermine the secular aspirations of his people. Then the premature revolt which Nasty feared breaks out. Nasty pleads with Goetz to save the situation he has created and make the revolt succeed by becoming the peasant's general. Goetz replies by telling Nasty that if he were to become a general again he would have to start hanging men again; for that was the secret of his discipline and his success. But now, he says, he lives only for love; and instead of listening to Nasty, he promises the saintly Christian Hilda that he will not shed blood. He goes to the peasants' camp, not to become their general, but to urge them to desist from fighting a war they cannot win, and to join with him in living for love alone. But the peasants only jeer at Goetz. In an excess of impatience, he curses them as swine. Afterwards he is filled with repentance and prays for divine guidance:

Here I am my God; here we are face to face again, as in the good old days when I was doing evil. Ah! I should never have interfered with men; they are a clog. They are the brushwood a man must part in order to come to You. I am coming, Lord, I come. I am walking in Your night; stretch out Your hand to help me ... cover me, devour my foul body, slip between my soul and myself and destroy me. I demand the catastrophe, the shame, and the loneliness of scorn, for man is made to destroy man in himself, and to open himself like a female to the huge dark body of the night.[4]

Goetz soon discovers that the rebel peasants have destroyed his "model village" because his people will not take up arms with them; so he goes into the forest—the wilderness?—to chastise the sins of man through his own flesh. He emerges to learn, from Heinrich, that the barons have scored the victory against the peasants' troops which Nasty predicted. Goetz feels he has failed; and Heinrich is there to confront him with his failure. Heinrich tells Goetz again that he is an impostor: "The orders you pretend to receive from God you give to yourself." Goetz reflects on this thought, and presently he says that he agrees with Heinrich:

I alone, priest, you are right. I alone. I supplicated. I demanded a sign, I sent messages to Heaven. No reply. Heaven ignored my very name. I demanded minute by minute what I could BE in the eyes of God. Now I know the answer: nothing. God does not see me, God does not hear me, God does not know me. You see this emptiness over our heads? That is God. You see this breach in the walls? It is God. You see that hole in the ground? That is God again. The silence is God. The absence is God. God is the loneliness of man. There was no one but myself; I alone decided on Evil; and I alone invented God. . . .

Heinrich tries to run away from Goetz, but he catches him and says:

Heinrich, I am going to tell you a colossal joke: God does not exist. He doesn't exist! Joy, tears of joy. Halleluia. Fool! Don't strike me, I have delivered us. No more Heaven, no more Hell; nothing but Earth.[5]

Goetz then goes back to Nasty and tells him "I want to be

a man among men." And he explains what that means: he must begin with crime:

Men of today are born criminals; I must demand my share in their crimes if I desire my share of their love and their virtue. I wanted love in all its purity. Ridiculous nonsense. To love a man is to hate the same enemy; therefore I will embrace your hatred. I wanted to do Good: foolishness. On this earth and at this time, Good and Evil are inseparable. I accept my share of Evil to inherit my share of Good.[6]

Nasty again offers Goetz the generalship of the peasants' army. He hesitates, but Nasty commands him to accept. Goetz puts on a uniform, and immediately issues an order that all deserters will be hanged:

A fine start. Nasty I told you I would be a hangman and butcher... Don't be afraid, I shan't flinch. I shall make them hate me because I know no other way of loving them. I shall give them their orders, since I have no other way of being obeyed. I shall remain alone with this empty sky above me, since I have no other way of being among men. There is this war to fight, and I will fight it.[7]

So *Le Diable et le bon Dieu* ends. I believe it to be a work of the highest art, for it is a play which transforms a particular problem in politics into one of the great moral dilemmas of mankind. This is drama on the scale of Sophocles' *Antigone*. Sartre has excelled himself. In *Les Mains sales* and *L'Engrenage*, both of which prefigure *Le Diable et le bon Dieu*, he matches a hard-headed socialist against a tender "bourgeois" conscience, which is seen as something small if not actually cowardly. In the present play the two sides of the conflict are better balanced. The way of non-violence and love and peaceful change is given its full moral force; the stigma of the "bourgeois" is no longer attached to it. There is thus a genuine and compelling alternative against which the "realist" socialist ethic has to vindicate itself. We are shown a bitter and lacerating struggle: the inner travail of one man projected and magnified into a massive tragedy.

One may discern in the piece, no doubt, the lineaments of Sartre's own political development. But one should not diminish the play by thinking of it as something meant to justify merely the author's attitude to Communism. Of course a defence of political ruthlessness can be read as a defence of the Communists' political ruthlessness; but the author's aim has not been to present the special predicament of twentieth-century socialism in a sixteenth-century guise; his subject is something which belongs to the whole of history. One might call his subject the politics of humanism; and the play's unmistakable message is that the politics of humanism must renounce the ethics of non-violence which belongs to the politics of religion and contemplation and quietism, the politics of the world to come. The politics of humanism is the politics of this world; and because this world is so deeply touched with evil (the consequence, on Sartre's view, of scarcity), to master it one must be ruthless, one must (for Sartre is not a man to mince his words) soil oneself with crime.*

I do not share this view but one can, I think, detect a remarkable resemblance between it and that of Machiavelli—not the immoralist of popular tradition, but the historical Machiavelli, who cared passionately for the regeneration of Italy, and who dreamed of a revival of the ancient Roman republican ideals of *virtù*, courage, magnanimity, and manliness to take the place of the

---

* In Jan. 1962, Sartre formed, with L. Schwartz and J.-P. Vigier, a second Left-wing movement, an Anti-Fascist League, having no detailed programme, but designed to "link the struggle against the O.A.S. with the struggle against the government and against personal power" (*France Observateur*, 1 Feb. 1962, p. 8). In a public statement on the aims of the League, Sartre said: "For me, *the essential problem* is to reject that theory according to which the Left ought not to answer violence with violence" (*op. cit.*, p. 7; my italics).

creeping, monkish ideals of humility, self-denial, non-resistance, patience, and prayer, which were taught by Christianity. To achieve the ends which he believed embodied the true glory of mankind, Machiavelli declared that it would sometimes be necessary to lie and cheat and kill. He did not wrap up his advice in the usual language of polite hypocrisy; he did not call killing "execution," or deceitfulness "diplomacy." Hence a great visionary is commonly traduced as a "cynic." Sartre has something of the same outspokenness. He does not look with Machiavelli to the republican virtues of Roman antiquity; his ideal is the classless society of Marx; but like Machiavelli he is less concerned with the structure of his better world than with the means of bringing it to birth; and like Machiavelli, he seeks to liberate his humanism from the moral inhibitions which derive from another ethos.

And yet there is a sense in which Sartre is conspicuously unlike Machiavelli. Machiavelli is the complete and unadulterated humanist; there is no admixture of religion in him. In Sartre there is. Indeed this is what makes him so effectively the dramatist, that he has at once a humanist intelligence and a religious sensibility, that he has always remained another Kierkegaard as well as another Hegel.

It is a religious sensibility which shrinks from the external world, and perceives it, as Sartre does, as entirely viscous, sticky, messy, sweetish, nauseating. The humanistic sensibility rejoices in nature; but Sartre sees natural objects as "vague," "soft," "flabby," "creamy," "thick," "tepid," "dull," "sickly," and "obscene." He is revolted also by women. There is something sickening about all the female characters in Sartre's plays and stories. Woman is seen as corrupt and corrupting; and in the very viscosity of the physical world, half-fluid, half-solid, Sartre discerns what is passive, yielding, and *feminine*. Sexual congress is invariably depicted by him as a

charmless exercise. If there is such a thing as a tender
heterosexual relationship in all Sartre's writings (something to compare with the homosexual relationship
between Brunet and Vicarios), it is between Charles, the
cripple on his trolley, holding hands in a train with
Catherine, a fellow-patient who has just defaecated near
him; humiliated, but *purged*, Catherine has the purity the
others lack. For the rest, the phrase of St. Bernard about
women being "bags of excrement" might well have been
spoken by Sartre.

The perfect order of astronomy, which spoke to Kant
and Newton of God, is an order for which Sartre's heart
hungers. What appeals to him is everything which is
opposed to viscosity: the hard, austere, metallic, mathe-
matical, predictable, inflexible, unsentimental, stern, and
masculine. The idea of "salvation through art," which has
so attracted him, is the idea of *overcoming* the messy,
disordered, contingent, sickening world of appearance by
creating a world of imagined order, perfection, necessity,
balance, poise and serenity. Equally, to think of art as a
means of salvation is to make art a kind of religion. And
undoubtedly as Sartre moved from the idea of salvation
through art to that of salvation through socialism, he was
moving from one form of religion to another.

Sartre once said that everyone is an atheist nowadays:
"God is dead, even for the believer." The reverse of this
is no less true; that an atheist of Sartre's kind makes God
live. The American Protestant theologian Paul Tillich
has introduced the name "The God above God" for the
God whose existence is affirmed by certain kinds of
doubt: "The God who is absent as an object of faith is
present as the source of restlessness which asks the ultimate question, the question of the meaning of existence."
Tillich goes on to say:

The absent God, the source of the question and the
doubt about himself is neither the God of theism nor of

pantheism; he is neither the God of the Christians nor
of the Hindus; he is neither the God of the naturalists
nor of the idealists. All these forms of the divine image
have been swallowed by the waves of radical doubt.
What is left is only the inner necessity of a man to ask
the ultimate question with complete seriousness. He
himself may not call the source of this inner necessity
God. He probably will not. But those who have had a
glimpse of the working of the divine Presence, know
that one could even ask the ultimate question without
this Presence, even if it makes itself felt only as the absence of God. The God above God is a name for God
who appears in the radicalism and the seriousness of
the ultimate question, even without an answer.[8]

Sartre might serve as a perfect illustration of Professor
Tillich's thesis; and readers who share Sartre's taste for
psycho-analytical literary criticism may look for a
connexion between the "God above God" and that
father-of-a-father who dominated Sartre's childhood. His
religious sensibility is such that as he has moved away
from the idea of "salvation through art," the aesthetic
merit of his writing has diminished. But the artist in him
has never been wholly swallowed up by the intellectual,
and in *Le Diable et le bon Dieu* he produced, at 47, at least
one play which is as good as the best of his early work.
Besides, what is important about Sartre is not only that
he has this unmistakably religious sensibility, but that
his sensibility has a polar antithesis in his rationalistic
intelligence. And if we resist Sartre's idea that all relationships between people are based on conflict, we must
at the same time admit that conflict is the stuff of drama;
and that conflict of another kind, in the sense of the
dialectic, is a large part of philosophy. And if some are
disappointed that Sartre's "ethics of deliverance" has
never been elaborated, and his search for salvation
transmuted into a short-term onslaught on the bourgeois

and a long-term attempt to revise the theoretical basis of socialism, we should none of us too readily hope for the conflicts in Sartre to end. For the sake of drama and philosophy we may wish him to continue to be held, in a phrase of Simone de Bauvoir, by "une tension constante."

REFERENCES

1. *M.S.*, p. 210 (95).
2. *L'Engrenage*, p. 187 (108)
3. *D.D.*, p. 139 (70).
4. *D.D.*, p. 235 (117).
5. *D.D.*, pp. 267–8 (132–3).
6. *D.D.*, p. 275 (137).
7. *D.D.*, p. 282 (141).
8. *Listener* (London), 3 Aug. 1961, p. 169.

BIBLIOGRAPHY

Note

*In all cases in which two or more editions of any work are listed,
all references in the text are to the editions marked * in this
Bibliography*

I. SARTRE

1 Philosophical, Critical, and Political Writings

L'Imagination. Paris (Presses Universitaires de France) 1936.

Esquisse d'une théorie des émotions. Paris (Hermann) 1939. Eng. translations: (1) *Outline of a Theory of the Emotions*, tr. Bernard Frechtman, Philosophical Library, New York 1948; (2) *Sketch for a
Theory of the Emotions*, tr. Philip Mairet, London (Methuen) 1962.

L'Imaginaire: psychologie phénoménologique de l'imagination. Paris (Gallimard) 1940. Eng. translation: *The Psychology of Imagination*, tr.
Bernard Frechtman, London (Rider) 1949.

L'Etre et le néant: essai d'ontologie phénoménologique. Paris (Gallimard)
1943. Eng. translation: *Being and Nothingness*, tr. Hazel Barnes,
New York (Philosophical Library) 1956; London (Methuen)
1957.

L'Existentialisme est un humanisme. Paris (Nagel) 1946. Eng. translations:
Existentialism, tr. Bernard Frechtman, New York (Philosophical
Library) 1947; *Existentialism and Humanism*, tr. Philip Mairet,
London (Methuen) 1948.

Réflexions sur le question juive. Paris (Morihien) 1946. Eng. translations:
(1) *Portrait of the Anti-Semite*, tr. Erik de Mauny, London
(Secker and Warburg) 1948; (2) *Anti-Semite and Jew*, tr. J.
Becker, New York (Shoeken) 1948.

Baudelaire. Paris (Gallimard) 1947. Eng. translation: *Baudelaire*, tr.
Martin Turnell, London (Horizon) 1949; New York (New
Directions) 1950.

Situations I. Paris (Gallimard) 1947. *Literary and Philosophical Essays*, tr.
Annette Michelson, London (Rider) 1955, contains most of the
essays in this volume, with others from later collections.

Situations II, Paris (Gallimard) 1948. This volume includes *Qu'est-ce
que la littérature?*, translated into English, as *What is Literature?*,
tr. Bernard Frechtman, New York (Philosophical Library) 1949;
London (Methuen) 1951.

Situations III. Paris (Gallimard) 1949.

Entretiens sur la politique. Paris (Gallimard) 1949.

116 SARTRE

Saint Genet, comédien et martyr. Paris (Gallimard) 1952.
L'Affaire Henri Martin. Paris (Gallimard) 1953.
Critique de la raison dialectique. Paris (Gallimard) 1960.

2. Novels and Short Stories

La Nausée. Paris (Gallimard) 1938. Eng. translation: *The Diary of Antoine Roquentin*, tr. Lloyd Alexander, *London (John Lehmann) 1949; *Nausea*, tr. Lloyd Alexander, New York (New Directions) 1949.

Le Mur. Contains the short stories "Le Mur," "La Chambre," "Erostrate," "Intimité," and "L'Enfance d'un chef." Paris (Gallimard) 1939. Eng. translation: *Intimacy*, tr. Lloyd Alexander, London (Neville Spearman) 1949; New York (New Directions) 1952; and *London (Panther Books) 1960.

L'Age de raison. Paris (Gallimard) 1945. Eng. translation: *The Age of Reason*, tr. Eric Sutton, London (Hamish Hamilton) 1947; New York (Knopf) 1947; and *Harmondsworth (Penguin) 1961.

Le Sursis. Paris (Gallimard) 1945. Eng. translation: *The Reprieve*, tr. Eric Sutton, *London (Hamish Hamilton) 1947; *Reprieve*, tr. Eric Sutton, New York (Knopf) 1947.

La Mort dans l'âme. Paris (Gallimard) 1949. Eng. translation: *Iron in the Soul*, tr. Gerard Hopkins, *London (Hamish Hamilton) 1950; *Troubled Sleep*, tr. Gerard Hopkins, New York (Knopf) 1951.

The three foregoing vols. belong to Sartre's unfinished tetralogy *Les Chemins de la liberté*. Two chapters of the projected fourth volume, *La Dernière chance*, were published as "Drôle d'amitié" in *Les Temps modernes*, Nov. and Dec. 1949.

3. Plays and Film Scenarios

Les Mouches. Paris. (Gallimard) 1943. Eng. translation: *The Flies*, in *Two Plays*, tr. Stuart Gilbert, London (Hamish Hamilton) 1946; *No Exit and the Flies*, tr. Stuart Gilbert, New York (Knopf) 1947.

Les Jeux sont faits. Paris (Nagel) 1946. Eng. translation: *The Chips are Down*, tr. Louise Varèse, London (Rider) 1951.

L'Engrenage. Paris (Nagel) 1946. Eng. translation: *In the Mesh*, tr. Mervyn Savill. London (Dakers) 1954.

Théâtre. Paris (Gallimard) 1947. Contains: *Les Mouches, Huis clos, Morts sans sépultures*, and *La Putain respectueuse*. Eng. translations: (1) *In Camera* (*Huis clos*), in *Two Plays*, tr. Stuart Gilbert, London (Hamish Hamilton) 1946; (2) *Men without Shadows* (*Morts sans sépulture*), and (3) *The Respectable* [sic] *Prostitute* (*La Putain respectueuse*), both in *Three Plays*, tr. Kitty Black, London (Hamish Hamilton) 1949. *Three Plays*, tr. Lionel Abel, New York (Knopf)

1949 includes *The Respectful Prostitute, Dirty Hands,* and *The Victors.*

Les Mains sales. Paris (Gallimard) 1948. Eng. translation: *Crime Passionnel,* in *Three Plays,* tr. Kitty Black, London (Hamish Hamilton) 1949; also published separately, *London (Methuen) 1961. See also *Three Plays,* tr. L. Abel.

Le Diable et le bon Dieu. Paris (Gallimard) 1951. Eng translation: *Lucifer and the Lord,* tr. Kitty Black, *London (Hamish Hamilton) 1953; *The Devil and the Good Lord,* tr. Kitty Black, with *Kean,* tr. Kitty Black, and *Nekrassov,* tr. S. and G. Leeson, New York (Knopf) 1960.

Kean, ou Désorde et génie (adapted from Alexandre Dumas's play). Paris (Gallimard) 1954. Eng. translation: *Kean, or Disorder and Genius,* tr. Kitty Black, London (Hamish Hamilton) 1954; with *The Devil and the Good Lord,* tr. Kitty Black, and *Nekrassov,* tr. S. and G. Leeson, New York (Knopf) 1960.

Nekrassov. Paris (Gallimard) 1956. English translation: *Nekrassov,* tr. Sylvia and George Leeson, London (Hamish Hamilton) 1946; with *The Devil and the Good Lord,* tr. Kitty Black, and *Kean,* tr. Kitty Black, New York (Knopf) 1960.

Les Séquestrés d'Altona. Paris (Gallimard) 1956. Eng. translation: *Loser Wins,* tr. Sylvia and George Leeson, London (Hamish Hamilton) 1960; *Condemned of Altona,* tr. S. and G. Leeson, New York (Knopf) 1961.

4. Miscellaneous Essays and Articles

"L'Existentialisme: mise au point." *Action* (Paris), 22 Dec. 1944.
"Forgers of Myths." *Théâtre-Arts* (Paris), Jul. 1946.
"American Novelists in French Eyes." *Atlantic Monthly* (Boston), Aug. 1946.
"Le Processus historique." *Gazette de Lausanne,* 9 Feb. 1947.
"C'est pour nous tous que sonne le glas." *Caliban* (Paris), Apr. 1948.
"Au Nick's Bar." *Caliban* (Paris), Jul. 1948.
"Avoir faim, c'est déjà vouloir être libre." *Caliban* (Paris), Oct. 1948.
"Jeunes d'Europe, unissez vous." *La Gauche* (Paris), Jun. 1948.
"De Partout on veut vous mystifier." *La Gauche* (Paris), Jul. 1948.
"Aux Marocains." *La Gauche* (Paris), Nov. 1948.
"Réponse à François Mauriac." *Le Figaro littéraire* (Paris), 7 May 1949.
"Les Jours de notre vie." *Les Temps modernes* (Paris), Jan. 1950.
"Gide vivant." *Les Temps modernes* (Paris), Mar. 1951.
"Sommes-nous en démocratie?" *Les Temps modernes* (Paris), Apr. 1952.
"Les Communistes et la paix." *Les Temps modernes,* Jul., Oct., and Nov. 1952, and Apr. 1954.

"Réponse à Albert Camus." *Les Temps modernes*, Aug. 1952.
"Réponse à Lefort." *Les Temps modernes*, Apr. 1953.
"Opération Kanapa." *Les Temps modernes*, Mar. 1954.
"Les Peintures de Giacometti." *Les Temps modernes*, Jun. 1954.
"Le Réformisme et les fétiches." *Les Temps modernes*, Feb. 1956.
"Le Colonialisme est un système." *Les Temps modernes*, Mar. and Apr. 1956.
"Le Fantôme de Staline." *Les Temps modernes*, Jan. 1957.
"Vous êtes formidables." *Les Temps modernes*, May 1957.
"Le Séquestré de Venise." *Les Temps modernes*, Nov. 1957.
"Nous sommes tous des assassins." *Les Temps modernes*, Mar. 1958.
"La Constitution du mépris." *L'Express* (Paris), 11 Sep. 1958.
"Camus." *France-Observateur* (Paris), 7 Jan. 1960.

II OTHERS

ALBÉRÈS, R. E.: *Sartre*. Paris (Editions Universitaires) 1954.
BEIGBEDER, MARC: *L'Homme Sartre*. Paris (Bordas) 1947.
BOUTANG, P. and PINGAUD, B.: *Sartre, est-il un possedé?*, Paris (Table Rond) 1946.
CAMPBELL, ROBERT: *Jean-Paul Sartre, ou une littérature philosophique*. Paris (Ardent) 1945.
DEMPSEY, PETER J. R.: *The Psychology of Sartre*, Cork 1950.
DESAN, WILFRID: *The Tragic Finale: An Essay on the Philosophy of Jean-Paul Sartre*. Cambridge (Harvard U.P.), Mass., 1954.
GREENE, NORMAN N.: *Jean-Paul Sartre: The Existentialist Ethic*. Ann Arbor (Univ. of Michigan Press) 1960.
JAMESON, FREDRIC: *Sartre, The Origins of a Style*, New Haven (Yale U.P.) 1961.
JEANSON, FRANCIS: *Le Problème moral et la pensée de Sartre*. Paris (Myrthe) 1947.
——: *Sartre par lui-même*. Paris (Seuil) 1954.
KNIGHT, EVERETT W.: *The Objective Society*. New York (Braziller) 1959.
MURDOCH, IRIS: *Sartre: Romantic Rationalist*. Cambridge (Bowes and Bowes), Eng., 1953; New Haven (Yale U.P.) 1953.
STERN, ALFRED: *Sartre: His Philosophy and Psychoanalysis*, New York (Liberal Arts Press) 1953.
†THODY, PHILIP: *Jean-Paul Sartre: A Literary and Political Study*. London (Hamish Hamilton) 1960; New York (Macmillan) 1961.

† The present author is indebted to Mr Thody's book for some information contained in this bibliography.